GST: A Transformational Tax Reform

V.S. Krishnan is a senior civil servant belonging to the Indian Revenue Service with wide experience in handling matters relating to Indirect Tax Policy. In the early part of his career he served as the Member of the Tax Research Unit, where he was associated with the formulation of four Union Budget. He has worked extensively on improving the Compliance Verification system through contributions to the preparation of the Audit Manual (under a Canadian Project) and a Return Scrutiny model (under the Asian Development Bank). He was conferred with the Presidential award for his Distinguished Record in 1999. He was closely associated with the evolution of the GST and was also Director on the board of GSTN.

GST: A Transformational Tax Reform

V.S. KRISHNAN

ACADEMIC FOUNDATION
NEW DELHI

www.academicfoundation.org

First published in 2018
by

ACADEMIC FOUNDATION
4772-73 / 23 Bharat Ram Road, (23 Ansari Road),
Darya Ganj, New Delhi - 110 002 (India).
Phones : 23245001 / 02.
Fax : +91-11-23245005.
E-mail : booksaf@gmail.com
www.academicfoundation.org

Disclaimer:
The opinions/views/findings expressed in this book are solely those of the authors and do not necessarily reflect the views of the publisher.

Cataloging in Publication Data--DK
Courtesy: D.K. Agencies (P) Ltd. <docinfo@dkagencies.com>

Krishnan, V. S., author.
GST : a transformational tax reform / V.S. Krishnan.
pages cm
ISBN 9789332704688

1. Value-added tax--India. 2. Value-added tax--Government policy--India. I. Title.

LCC HJ5715.I4K75 2018 | DDC 336.27140954 23

Typeset, printed and bound by The Book Mint, New Delhi.
www.thebookmint.in

Dedicated to the officers of the Central Board of Indirect Taxes and Customs (CBIC), the officers and staff of the Commercial Tax Department of the various State Governments and officials of the GSTN who carried the GST project successfully on their shoulders.

Contents

III
Policy Prescriptions Going Forward

IV
Annexures and Appendices

List of Tables and Figures

Tables

Figures

अरुण जेटली
वित्त एवं कार्पोरेट कार्य मंत्री
भारत

सत्यमेव जयते

Arun Jaitley
Minister of Finance and Corporate Affairs
India

26th March, 2018

FOREWORD

This book written by Mr. V.S. Krishnan is both timely and topical. As an erstwhile Member of the Board of Central Excise and Customs, Mr. Krishnan had a ringside view of the evolution of the GST. The book is written in a very lucid and readable style and would be useful to the lay reader to understand the essence of GST. In the latter half of the book, a number of interesting suggestions have been made from the policy perspective. I am sure that this book will be useful for both the lay reader and the tax professional.

(Arun Jaitley)

Office : 134, North Block, New Delhi-110001, Tel. : 23092810, 23092510 Fax : 23092828
Residence : 2, Krishna Menon Marg, New Delhi-110011, Tel. : 23794990, 23794556 Fax : 23794543

Acknowledgement

The GST has been described by many as a transformational tax reform. Some have called it India's second tryst with destiny. The undersigned was fortunate to participate in many of the GST deliberations and serve also as a member of various sub-committees on GST. The motivation behind writing this book was to share the GST story with the lay public. Its evolution in a multi-party democracy is a great example of cooperation federalism at its best. In writing this book, I have greatly benefited from my conversations with my brother Dr Arvind Subramanian who provided me with many illuminating insights about GST at a conceptual level. I am also thankful to Shanti Sundaram, former Chairman of the Central Board of Indirect Taxes and Customs (CBIC), formerly known as Central Board of Excise and Customs (CBEC), who nominated me to a crucial subcommittee on "Dual Control, Rates and Exemption" which was created by the Empowered Committee of State Finance Minister during their meeting in 2005-06 at Bhubaneswar. The deliberations in this committee which had representatives of State governments was extremely enjoyable and helped me to look at issues from the perspective of the States.

I am also grateful to my former colleagues Upendra Gupta and Ravneet Singh who worked with me in the GST Policy Group. Their domain knowledge helped me to understand the intricate details of the GST.

I am also thankful to Prakash Kumar, CEO, Goods and Services Tax Network (GSTN), who provided me with useful insights about the technological challenge in relation to GST during my stint as the CBIC nominee on the GSTN Board.

While I have mentioned a few names there are large number of young and bright officers who have worked very hard, away from the glare of publicity. This book is my humble offering to all these officers of the Indian Revenue Service whose efforts have made the GST happen.

— V.S. Krishnan

Introduction

The motivation to write this book sprang from my fortunate association with a large number of tax reforms as a member of the Indian Revenue Service. I was a member of the Tax Research Unit in the 1980s when 'MODVAT' credit was introduced as part of the reform of the Central Excise regime to offset the cascading effect of tax on tax. This was followed by a number of reforms, including rationalisation of tax rates and introduction of invoice based assessment which sought to bring in a number of features of the Central GST. The introduction of Service Tax in 1994 was another step in the GST journey for the Central government.

I was a member of the Sub-committee on Dual Control, Threshold and Exemptions created by the Empowered Committee of State Finance Ministers at their Bhubaneswar conference. The deliberations of the committee provided insights into the thinking of the States about the GST. As a Member (GST) later in 2015 in the CBIC, I was associated with the drafting of the GST legislation. As a core GST member in the CBIC, it was fascinating to watch the GST reform unfold.

This book explores the evolution of the GST story in all its facets. It was an audacious attempt to integrate the State and Central VAT into a GST which would span the entire spectrum of the value chain. The Chief Economic Advisor described this quite eloquently:

To have achieved this, in a large and complex federal system of multiparty democracy, with a Centre, 29 States and 2 Union Territories of widely divergent interests via a constitutional amendment requiring broad political consensus, affecting potentially 7.5 million tax entities, and marshalling the latest technology to use and improve tax implementation capability, is perhaps breathtakingly unprecedented in modern global tax history.

The only near parallel is the Aadhar project which provided an identity number with biometric details for 1.25 billion Indians. Even this project however will fail to match the complexity of the GSTN endeavour.

The book looks at the remarkable GST journey in three parts. Part I explores the evolution of the GST story including the debates that shaped the GST. Part II examines the implementation of the GST and its impact. Finally, Part III looks at the policy prescriptions required going forward. The book suggests that the GST is still a work in progress and many policy changes would be required going forward to make what is a 'good GST a great GST'. Like many reforms the GST will throw up transitional challenges including the technical challenge of managing the GSTN network which provides technical support to the GST.

The GSTN itself is one of the most audacious IT projects undertaken which can even challenge the Aadhar project in its complexity. Besides providing a common online portal for all businesses to carry out three core business processes—registration, payment of duty and submission of returns, the GSTN will also match more than 3 billion invoices of buyers and suppliers every month according to the information given by the GSTN management.

This book has been written in the hope that the lay reader will get a flavour of the transformational aspects of the GST reform.

I
Evolution of GST

1

The GST Story

The VAT (value added tax) was conceptualised by a German businessman Georg Wilhelm von Siemens in the year 1920. The year is historically significant for it was the period just after the end of World War I which debilitated much of Europe. Economists were exploring various avenues for raising revenues to support the expenditure demands of war ravaged economies, seeking to rebuild. Germany was in the forefront of these efforts driven by sheer economic necessity.

The VAT idea originally conceived by von Siemens was further refined by Maurice Lauré who was the pioneer in the introduction of modern VAT in France in 1948. From France, it went to the colonies in Western Africa and subsequently to South America. It entered Europe aided by the process of economic integration of the European Union. However, VAT gained real popularity in the 1980s and 1990s and was universally adopted with the notable exception of the United States. Table 1.1 gives the regional spread of VAT.

What really explains the popularity of VAT which caught the fiscal imagination of the world?

The answer lies probably in its simplicity and the administrative ease of collection.

In their book titled, *The Modern VAT*, Ebrill, Keen, Bodin and Summers[1] have defined the VAT as a "broad based tax levied on commodity sales up to and including at

1. Ebrill, L., M. Keen, J-P Bodin, and V. Summers (2001). *The Modern VAT*. Washington DC: IMF.

least the manufacturing stage, with systematic offsetting of tax on commodities purchased as input against that due on outputs".

Table 1.1

Regional Spread of VAT

Year	*Sub-Saharan Africa*	*Asia & Pacific*	*EU (plus Norway & Switzerland)*	*Central Europe & Baltic Region*	*North Africa & Middle*	*Americas*	*Small Islands*
2001 (April)	27 (43)	18 (24)	17 (17)	25 (26)	6 (21)	22 (26)	8 (27)
1989	4	6	15	1	4	16	1
1979	1	1	12	0	1	12	0
1969	1	0	5	0	0	2	0

Note: The figure in brackets is the total number of countries in each region.

Source: IMF calculations.

So VAT really started as MANVAT or as a VAT on manufacturing, but later expanded to services and covered the entire value chain. Today because VAT taxes value addition in both goods and services—it is also called the 'Goods and Service Tax (GST)'. It really works on the principle that all value addition must be treated on par whether it be in hair clips or haircuts. Various tax experts have lauded this mainly on the premise that it is comprehensive in its coverage and taxes the entire value chain. This in turn permits lower rates of taxes.

There are a number of ways in which value addition can be taxed. Broadly speaking, we can have three methods:

(i) Tax on output–Tax on input: This is called the invoice credit method, for tax paid at each point of the production and distribution chain is captured on the invoice and this document is used as the basis for allowing the offsetting of input tax against output tax. This method is commonly used and popularised by the original EEC model later spreading to Africa and then to Asia.

(ii) Taxes on wages+Profit: This is also known as the additive method and is levied on value added calculated by adding factor incomes.

(iii) Tax is also levied directly based on the accounts of the company by subtracting allowable purchases from revenue. This method is also popularly known as the subtractive method. The method explained can be expressed as: Tax (output–input).

The essential popularity of the GST can be ascribed to its revenue efficiency.

What really enhances the revenue efficiency of VAT is that the collection of revenue is made at many points rather than only at the last stage, as under RST (retail sales tax), which renders the retail sales tax more vulnerable to evasion. This aspect is brought out very lucidly in the example relating to steel industry given in Table 1.2.

Table 1.2

Equivalence to 10 Per cent VAT and 10 Per cent RST (in ₹)

	Value	*VAT on Purchase*	*VAT on Sale*	*VAT to Government*	*Value Added*	*Retail Price*	*RST*
Iron Ore	100	-	10	10	100	-	-
Steel sheet	130	10	13	3	30	-	-
Finished steel	160	13	16	3	30	-	-
Steel plate (Manuf.)	200	16	20	4	40	-	-
Steel plate (Retail)	250	20	25	5	50	-	-
Total	250	-	-	25	-	275	25

Source: Extracted from Shome, Parathasarathi (2002). *India's Fiscal Matters*. Oxford University Press.

As can be seen from Table 1.2, the tax collected both under VAT and RST is the same, viz., ₹25 (comparison between total VAT to Government and RST). However, the point is that if the retailer is not brought into the tax net, the entire revenue of ₹25 would be lost. On the other hand, the VAT is collected as an accumulation of tax at each stage (iron ore ₹10, steel sheet ₹3, finished steel ₹3, steel plate (manufactured) ₹4, steel plate (retail) ₹5). The revenue efficiency of VAT explained above is corroborated by the difference in revenue realised from VAT and the predecessor retail sales tax.

The revenue efficiency of VAT was experienced by many of the countries who implemented this. Table 1.3 shows the impact.

Table 1.3

Revenue Difference between VAT and Predecessor Sales Tax by Region

	Sub-Saharan Africa	*Asia & Pacific*	*Americas*	*EU (plus Norway & Switzerland)*	*North Africa & Middle East*	*Small Islands*
Growth rate	1.10	0.70	1.42	1.05	0.10	1.96

Source: Compiled by the author.

Table 1.3 clearly shows that there have been significant revenue gains across the regions.

Global Practice

If we look at the VAT system around the world, we find that most of the countries have gone by the invoice credit method which provides an invoice trail right across the value chain. This has helped to enhance the revenue efficiency of the tax. The design of the GST (VAT) varies from country to country, ranging from a unitary VAT system in the European Union (EU) to a dual VAT in Brazil and Canada. Table 1.4 briefly describes the design of the GST in terms of the levy of VAT by the Central Federal Units and the States.

As we can see, countries in the EU like France have a single unified VAT. China also has a centralised VAT and revenues collected are shared with the Provinces. The United States does not have VAT but States levy RST on goods like liquor and tobacco.

Canada and Brazil have a dual GST system. In Canada considerable fiscal flexibility is given to the States to decide their own tax rates. Rates on commodities also vary from state to state making for non-uniformity of commodity taxation and also creating different taxable bases. In Brazil, some interstate transactions are taxed on the origin principle thereby diluting the equity advantages of a destination based tax. Brazil also assigns revenue from selective services like urban real estates at rates ranging between 2 to 5 per cent, to the local bodies including municipalities. This is an interesting practice

Table 1.4

Country-wise Design of the GST

Country	*Design of the GST*	*Remarks*
France	First country to introduce unified tax regime in 1954	—
USA	Does not impose any centralised VAT and the imposition of the VAT is left to the States	—
China	Centralised VAT: Revenue sharing with Provinces	—
Canada	Dual GST system, where revenues is divided between Centre and States	Canada broadly has a dual VAT system but States have flexibility to impose their own rates of harmonised sales tax. Thus the GST comprises a federal component as well as a provincial component, but certain provinces levy RST which is in the nature of single stage sales tax. Quebec province applies its own version of the VAT and treats financial services distinctly.
Brazil	Dual GST system where revenues is divided between Centre and States	The main state level tax is the consumption tax on merchandise and services (ICMS). The tax rates vary across States and commodities, from 0% to 25%. States also impose a tax on selected services such as telecom and interstate transport, as mandated by the Constitution. States impose a tax on motor vehicles (IPVA) at 3% of the market value. Interstate transactions are taxed partially at the origin, and partially at the destination. The rates vary; if trade is from a rich to poor state, it is taxed at 7% at the origin stage, in other cases, at 12%. Lower tax rates are applied on intrastate sales than on interstate sales, as would be expected for promotion of internal trade. The system allows for input tax credit in the importing state for taxes paid in the exporting state.
Germany	Centre controls policy formulation and States collect taxes	—
Australia	GST is a federal tax, collected by the central authority and later divided among the states	—

Source: Compiled by the author.

which India could emulate for it would strengthen the finances of our local bodies both the *panchayats* and the local urban corporations. Financial empowerment could facilitate qualitative improvements through facilitating local investments in priority sector like infrastructure, health and education.

In conclusion, GST addresses the classic dilemma faced by every tax department namely, how to balance revenue efficiency with administrative convenience. This was pithily described by Jean Baptist Colbert, Louis XIV's Minister of Treasury:

> The art of taxation consists in so plucking the goose as to obtain the largest amount of feathers with the smallest amount of hissing.

The evolution of the Indian GST story is described in the next chapter.

2

The Indian GST Story

The evolution of the Indian GST began as parallel initiatives taken by the Centre and the State to avoid the cascading effect of tax on tax. The policy reforms were taken at different ends of the value chain in view of the constitutional provisions which empowered the Centre to tax manufacturing and States to tax trading. The value addition in services was taxed under the residual financial powers vested with the Centre under the Constitution. Service Tax was introduced in 1994, 50 years after Central Excise Duty were consolidated under a Central law in 1944.

Centre's Journey Towards GST

The Indirect Taxation Committee headed by L.K. Jha examined the issue in the late 1970s and did recommend the introduction of VAT in the manufacturing part of the value chain calling it MANVAT (manufacturing value added tax) which was constitutionally in the centre's fiscal domain. In the 1990s, a series of measures taken by the Central government laid the ground work for the conversion of Central Excise Duty into a Central VAT (value added tax). First was the introduction of invoice based assessment moving away from the concept of deemed normal price to transaction value and widening of the input set-off credit scheme to cover most of the manufacturing items. The Central Board of Indirect Taxes and Customs (CBIC) also abolished the maintenance of statutory records, especially for larger companies and ruled that financial records maintained by large companies in the ordinary course of their business would be acceptable as statutory departmental records. This important policy pronouncement set the stage later for the introduction of audit based control.

More importantly in 1994, the service tax was imposed by the Centre drawing upon the fiscal powers vested under the residuary list in the Constitution. This was important because if GST was to be implemented, value addition in both goods and services would have to be integrated. The implementation of service tax duty began with the introduction of levy on three specific services, namely telecom, non-life insurance, and stock brokers. This later encompassed in 2012 all services except for services contained in the negative list. In the 1990s and 2000, the slow integration of CENVAT credits and procedures was initiated including the very important step of having a common registration number based on the PAN.

States Journey Towards GST

Introduction of VAT in the States has been a more challenging exercise in a federal country like India, where each State, in terms of the Constitutional provision, is sovereign in levying and collecting state taxes. Before introduction of VAT, in the sales tax regime, apart from the problem of multiple taxation and burden of adverse cascading effect of taxes as already mentioned, there was also no harmony in the rates of sales tax on different commodities among the States. Not only were the rates of sales tax numerous (often more than 10 in several States), and different from one another for the same commodity in different States, there was also an unhealthy competition among the States in terms of sales tax rates—so-called 'rate war'—often resulting in all round revenue reduction. This happened mainly to attract investments, but was counterproductive for it was a race to the bottom.

It is in this background that attempts were made by the States to introduce a harmonious VAT, while maintaining the sovereignty of the States in matters of taxation. The first preliminary discussion on State-level VAT took place in a meeting of Chief Ministers convened by Dr Manmohan Singh, the then Union Finance Minister in 1995. In this meeting, the basic issues on VAT were discussed in general terms and this was followed up by periodic interactions between State Finance Ministers. Thereafter, in a significant meeting of all the Chief Ministers, convened on 16 November 1999 by Yashwant Sinha, the then Union Finance Minister, two important decisions were taken. First, the introduction of state-level VAT would have to be preceded by the end of unhealthy sales tax 'rate war' among the States. The sales tax rates would therefore need to be harmonised by implementing uniform floor rates of sales tax for different categories of commodities with effect from 1 January 2000. Second, on the basis of achievement of the first objective, steps would have to be taken by the states for introduction of State-level VAT after adequate preparation. For implementing these decisions, a Standing Committee of State Finance Ministers was formed which then morphed into the Empowered Committee of State Finance Ministers.

The creation of the Empowered Committee of State Finance Minister's in 2001 and its registration under the Society Act in 2004 enacted a unique institution which was able to harmonise the VAT design for the States. This institution provided a forum for the States to voice their opinion which was very helpful in the reform of the VAT and later in the design of the GST. Its effectiveness was also enhanced by the tradition started by Yashwant Sinha of appointing a Finance Minister from an opposition-ruled state to head the Empowered Committee—a case of empowerment of the States by delegating management to the political adversary. The efforts also got a significant support from the then Finance Minister, P. Chidambaram who offered Centre's financial support to States in the event of a revenue loss during the transition phase to GST. As a result of these measures, the States started implementing VAT on 1 April 2005. Thanks to the effective monitoring of the Empowered Committee of

State Finance Minister's the deviation from the agreed VAT rate was contained to less than 3 per cent of the total list of commodities. Remarkably, the rate of growth of tax revenues was nearly double the average annual rate of growth after the introduction of VAT in comparison to the average revenue growth in the five year period of pre VAT.

Movement Towards GST

Emboldened by the success of VAT in States, the Centre initiated steps to implement a national GST, which would bring together the Central VAT and the State VAT covering the entire value chain.

The first step in creating this national framework for the GST was initiated by an Empowered Committee, setup under the chairmanship of Dr Asim Dasgupta, former Finance Minister of West Bengal and an economist of repute. This committee was asked to look at three sets of issues: (a) design issues, (b) operational issues, and (c) infrastructure issues. The creation of the empowered committee was initiated by the Thirteenth Finance Committee under the chairmanship of Dr Vijay Kelkar which also appointed a Task Force to advise the commission on the implementation of the GST. The deliberations of the Empowered Committee of State Finance Ministers and the recommendations of the Task Force were crystallised in the first Discussion Paper on Goods and Services Tax which was released on November 2009. One of the important items in the Terms of Reference of Thirteenth Finance Commission was "the impact of the proposed implementation of the goods and service tax with effect from 1 April 2010 including its impact on the country's foreign trade".

The discussion paper laid down the framework of dual GST. These were broadly the following:

(1) Consistent with the federal structure of the country, the GST will have two components: one levied by the Centre (hereinafter referred to as Central GST—CGST), and the other levied by the States (hereinafter referred to as State GST—SGST). This dual GST model would be

implemented through multiple statutes (one for CGST and SGST statute for every State). However, the basic features of law such as chargeability, definition of taxable event and taxable person, measure of levy including valuation provisions, basis of classification etc., would be uniform across these statutes as far as practicable.

(2) The CGST and the SGST would be applicable to all transactions of goods and services except the exempted goods and services, goods which are outside the purview of GST and the transactions which are below the prescribed threshold limits.

(3) The CGST and SGST are to be paid to the accounts of the Centre and the States separately.

(4) Since the CGST and SGST are to be treated separately, in general, taxes paid against the CGST shall be allowed to be taken as ITC (input tax credit) for the CGST and could be utilised only against the payment of CGST. The same principle will be applicable for the SGST.

(5) Cross utilisation of ITC between the CGST and the SGST would, in general, not be allowed.

(6) To the extent feasible, uniform procedure for collection of both CGST and SGST would be prescribed in the respective legislation for CGST and SGST.

(7) The administration of the CGST would be with the Centre and for SGST with the States.

(8) The taxpayer would need to submit periodical returns to both the CGST authority and to the concerned SGST authorities.

(9) Each taxpayer would be allotted a PAN linked taxpayer identification number with a total of 13/15 digits. This would bring the GST PAN-linked system in line with the prevailing PAN-based system for income tax facilitating data exchange and taxpayer compliance. The exact

design would be worked out in consultation with the Income Tax Department; and

(10) Keeping in mind the need of tax payer convenience, functions such as assessment, enforcement, scrutiny and audit would be undertaken by the authority which is collecting the tax, with information sharing between the Centre and the States.

The GST which has been implemented with effect from 1 July 2017, embodies all the broad features outlined in the first discussion paper and are contained in the 122nd Constitutional Amendment Act. While many may carp and complain about the flaws in the GST, there is no doubt that this is an audacious tax reform undertaken by the Centre, jointly in collaboration with 29 states and 2 Union Territories, within a federal system of multi-party democracy. The Chief Economic Advisor put this thought quite eloquently:

> The time is ripe to collectively seize this historic opportunity; not just because the GST will decisively alter the Indian economy for the better but also because the GST symbolises Indian politics and democracy at its cooperative, consensual best.

In the next chapter, we will examine the debates that shaped the GST and influenced its essential features.

3

Debates that Shaped the GST

The GST journey really began with the announcement by the finance minister in the Union Budget of 2008-09 that the GST would be implemented from 1 April 2010. The finance minister also outlined the approach stating that the roadmap for introduction of the GST would be shaped by the Central government in consultation with the States whose views would be reflected by an institutional body like the Empowered Committee of State Finance Ministers which delivered and monitored the implementation of the State VAT.

The period between 2008-09 and 2016-17 saw some interesting ideas being debated. These debates reflected the concerns of the States especially their fears about revenue loss and also the purported loss of fiscal sovereignty. The Centre on the other hand was anxious that the GST implemented should not be a moth-eaten GST but a full blown GST which would deliver all the advantages of the GST. The interaction between the Centre and the States in various forums demonstrated the vigour and vitality of our federal multi-party democracy.

Broadly the debates centred around the following issues:

(1) compensation to the States—the magnitude of revenue loss after implementation of GST;

(2) role and design of the institutional body which will represent the interest of the States;

(3) the design of the GST in terms of the items to be included and excluded;

(4) tax treatment of inter-sate trade transactions; and

(5) issue of cross empowerment of Centre and State tax officials for carrying out compliance verification.

Compensation

The implementation of GST was debated hotly on the issue of compensation. The States especially the manufacturing States like Maharashtra, Gujarat, and Tamil Nadu feared a revenue loss due to the abolition of CST visualised in the GST. The CST being an origin based tax the richer manufacturing States got the benefits of revenue collected at the point of origin for the supplies made to other States. The importance of the CST revenue can be gauged from Table 3.1.

Out of total revenue of ₹4,02,192.1 crore in 2016-17, nearly 39 per cent of revenues went to the richer states like Maharashtra, Gujarat and Tamil Nadu.

A lot of these revenues are expected to move to poorer, high consumption States like Bihar and Uttar Pradesh for GST is a destination based tax. Under pressure from States like Gujarat, the Centre contemplated first the imposition of 1 per cent additional tax on GST which would be non-offsetable and levied on goods traded inter-state. The Gujarat's justification was that they needed to be compensated for all the investments made by them for facilitating more investment in manufacturing. This idea was widely criticised by economists as representing a back door entry of CST again. Before the presentation of 122nd Constitution amendment bill for bringing its GST bill, there were hectic parleys between the Government and the industry which ultimately culminated in the dropping of this idea.

There was however the larger issue which remained namely the trust deficit between the Centre and the States on the payment of the compensation. This trust deficit had its roots in the purported non-payment of compensation to the States on account of reduction in

Table 3.1

State-wise CST Revenue, 2014-15 to 2016-17

(₹ *in crores*)

S. No.	*State*	*2014-15*	*2015-16*	*2016-17*
1	Gujarat	57265.3	47564.1	61344.5
2	Maharashtra	56685.8	47298.1	53522.5
3	Tamil Nadu	38551.2	41818.6	40914.5
4	Uttar Pradesh	17758.6	35665.3	41736
5	Haryana	16309.6	31423.4	29754.9
6	Karnataka	32518.9	18641.8	23698
7	West Bengal	15471	17172.1	20263.9
8	Rajasthan	15250.2	16150	16150
9	Chhattisgarh	9323.6	18373.6	18853.5
10	Jharkhand	10273.2	13717.2	17480.7
11	Telangana	14612.2	10955.2	14120
12	Andhra Pradesh	14882.2	11416.4	13013.8
13	Madhya Pradesh	10235.2	11593.7	12753.1
14	Odisha	9246.2	9535.9	9731
15	Assam	5268.3	6632.8	8350.7
16	Punjab	5569.6	5100	5620
17	Kerala	4644.3	3831.1	4784.1
18	Himachal Pradesh	4221.4	3212	5284.1
19	Uttarakhand	6473.1	-	-
20	Meghalaya	601.2	2540.1	1333.6
21	Goa	949.1	1288.6	2000
22	Bihar	653.8	816.9	1123.2
23	Sikkim	285.1	360	360
24	Tripura	29.7	-	-
25	Mizoram	-	0.3	-
26	Arunachal Pradesh	-	-	-
27	Jammu and Kashmir	-	-	-
28	Manipur	-	-	-
29	Nagaland	-	-	-
	Total	347078.8	402192.1	402192.1

Source: Compiled by the author.

the CST rates from 4 per cent to 2 per cent in the Union Budget of 2009-10. The payment of compensation for a limited period was justified by the then finance minister on the ground that this commitment was contingent on the implementation of the GST and was for a limited period and not free ended. It is here that the finance minister, Mr Jaitley played a stellar role in reaching out to the States. The first step then was to immediately release the amount to the States due to the CST rate reduction. A total compensation amount of ₹26,000 crore overdue to the states due to the reduction of CST rates was given to the State in two instalments during 2015-16 and 2016-17. This action reduced the trust deficit and facilitated a wider conversation between the Centre and the States. The States based on their past experience however insisted that the payment of compensation should come with a constitutional guarantee which alone would give the States some revenue confidence. The back and forth negotiation and debates culminated in the Centre agreeing to include this guarantee of compensation in the Constitution amendment bill itself. The States were promised compensation for the revenue loss for a period of five years from the date of implementation. The mandatory nature of the compensation was also fortified by the use of the expression 'shall' instead of 'may'. At the GST Council meeting the ground rules for giving this compensation were finalised in a highly accommodative manner. The Centre's compensation offer was generous for it promised a normative growth rate of 14 per cent in revenues reckoned on the taxable base of 2014-16. Incentives given by the State governments were however kept out of the definition of the taxable base. The successful closure of the compensation issue really set the tone for the implementation of the GST. The spirit in which the discussions were closed reflected the spirit of cooperative federalism.

Role and Design of the Institutional body

The Thirteenth Finance Commission headed by Dr Vijay Kelkar created a Task Force on GST which submitted its report on 15 December 2009. One of the recommendations of the Task Force was to transform the Empowered Committee of State Finance Ministers which was created to enforce the State VAT, into a permanent constitutional body known as the Council of Finance Ministers. The relevant extract of the Task Force give us an idea of the background of the creation of the GST council.

> The Council should be responsible for any modification in the initial design of the dual GST and regulating the indirect tax system in the country. The initial design of the dual GST should be approved by the Chairman and three-fourth of the State Finance Ministers. Thereafter, any change in the structure of the GST (both base and the rates) should be allowed to be carried out only if the Chairman and two-thirds of the State Finance Ministers agree to do so. Consequently, neither the Centre nor any state will have the authority to unilaterally make any change in the agreed design of the GST. However, in the event of a crisis, the Member State or the Centre may take immediate steps to impose a surcharge to ex-post facto approval by the Council within one month. Further, such surcharge should not be allowed to remain in force beyond a period of one year. This Council should, in due course, have a permanent secretariat of its own in New Delhi. The proposed mechanism will also ensure that all changes are thoroughly analysed and debated before being implemented. More importantly, since both the Centre and the States would surrender their individual autonomy to change the structure of the GST to the proposed Constitutional body, the existing balance of federal fiscal powers will continue to be maintained. Further, with a view to compensating for the perceived erosion in the tax anatomy of the States, we also recommend that there should be an increase in the formula-based devolution to the States.

This recommendation initiated widespread debate. Some of the smaller States especially the north eastern States felt that their voices could be silenced by the larger States seeking to protect their own interests. Some States like Tamil Nadu suggested that all the States should not have uniform voting rights based on the principle of one State one vote instead the value of the vote of each State should be proportional either to the population or to the States ratio of GDP in the total national GDP. This suggestion again was not acceptable to the Centre and many of the smaller States. Finally in the 115th Constitutional Amendment Bill moved by United Progressive Alliance (UPA) 2, the draft stated that the decisions taken by the council on any matters relating to rates and exemptions would be through a consensus rather than through voting. Many felt that the use of the word 'consensus' would make it very difficult to take any decision, for policy could be stymied by a few dissenting voices. Consensus would require unanimity which would be difficult to forge. The impracticality of this led to the Centre and the States agreeing to a new formula that all decisions would have to be approved by three-fourth of the GST council members which meant going back to the original recommendation of the Task Force.

The 122nd Constitutional amendment bill was passed and provided for decision by three-fourths majority in the council. This ensured that neither the Centre nor the States could unilaterally take any decision without coming together. A substantial number of States would have to support the Centre and vice versa if any decision was to be carried. This was at the end a happy compromise which entrenched the idea of cooperative federalism. What was really very reassuring was that in the end all the major decisions taken by the Council was through a consensus without having to go through a vote. A lot of credit for this need to go to the finance minister whose statesman like approach in reaching out to the States ensured that fine traditions had been set for the GST council going forward.

The powers of the GST council were specifically enumerated in Article 279A of the 122nd Constitution Amendment Act. The GST council was empowered to make recommendations to Centre and the States on the following matters:

(1) the taxes, cesses and surcharges levied by the Union, the States and the local bodies which may be subsumed in the GST;

(2) the goods and services that may be subjected to, or exempted from the goods and services tax;

(3) model GST laws, principles of levy, apportionment of GST levied on supplies in the course of inter-State trade or commerce under article 269A and the principles that govern the place of supply;

(4) the threshold limit of turnover below which goods and services may be exempted from GST;

(5) the rates including floor rates with bands of GST;

(6) any special rate or rates for a specified period, to raise additional resources during any natural calamity or disaster;

(7) special provision with respect to the States of Arunachal Pradesh, Assam, Jammu & Kashmir, Manipur, Meghalaya, Mizoram, Nagaland, Sikkim, Tripura, Himachal Pradesh, and Uttarakhand; and

(8) any other matter relating to the GST, as the Council may decide.

Taxable Base in the GST

The sectors to be included the taxable base under the GST was a matter of much debate right from the outset. The state resisted the inclusion of the petroleum and alcohol within the ambit of the GST. The Task Force set up by Thirteenth Finance Commission had recommended the idea of a 'flawless GST' (flawless because all sectors were included in GST taxable base). The Task Force recommended a revenue neutral rate of 12 per cent with all the important sectors forming part of GST including petroleum and real estate. The revenue diffidence of States however held the ground in the number of discussions. The States agreed to bring petroleum within GST which was a significant achievement but it was also decided that five items namely, diesel, petrol, crude oil, natural gas, and aviation turbine fuel would be kept out of the GST temporarily and would be exempt from GST and would be subject to prevailing excise duty rates to be levied as usual by the Centre and the States. Similarly, alcohol was also kept out of the GST. This ring fenced almost 40 per cent of the Centre's and States revenues from the impact of GST. One can therefore hope that if revenue collections are buoyant going forward, then these items could become part of the GST. On electricity, there was no constitutional bar for bringing it under the GST. The State's worry however was that inclusion of electricity may increase the tariff burden on consumers. This is a misplaced fear for inclusion of electricity would make manufacturing viable as embedded taxes amount to nearly 9 per cent of the tariff value. On real estate there was a vibrant debate. The Chief Economic Advisor vociferously argued for inclusion of the real estate and electricity within the ambit of the GST. On real estate, he argued that it would not be necessary to amend the definition of 'goods' in the Constitution in order to bring real estate within the ambit of GST. Real estate including land and building could be treated as a supply of a service. The artificial distinction which prevailed under the Service Tax between work contract services and services rendered in relation to construction of residential or commercial buildings could be removed. This would clean up the land markets which was a source of generation of black money income. This view was also vigorously supported by the Delhi Finance Minister Manish Sisodia. Finally, it was decided that this issue would be revisited after a year. On alcohol also some States like Tamil Nadu argued that these should be kept out of GST. Here, revenue considerations carried the day. In some cases, states view were accepted as a concession to their ceding their fiscal sovereignty.

Ultimately the GST design did not include real estate, alcohol and electricity, and also temporarily kept out five petroleum products. In some sense therefore based on the Kelkar benchmark this was a 'flawed GST'. But as the saying goes sometimes "best is the enemy of the good." The general feeling was that the GST should be implemented first regardless of some warts and subsequent improvement could be made as the system stabilises and revenue flows in. So in some sense pragmatism prevailed in the design of the GST.

Tax Treatment of Inter-state Transactions

The tax treatment of inter-state transaction was an important issue which needed to be resolved, for here the Centre and the State had different views. The Centre was of the view that given the constitutional position, the taxation of inter-state services fell under the fiscal domain of the Centre and therefore should be levied and collected by the Centre. The States on the other hand cited the example of the central sales tax where the States collected the tax on behalf of the Centre on the basis of delegation of power.

In the course of this debate three alternative model were suggested and discussed. First was the approach followed by the EU in which interstate transaction are zero rated and the refunds of the input credit both CGST and SGST would be given back to the supplier of goods. For example, if soap was supplied from Maharashtra to a dealer in Karnataka, zero rating of soap would imply no charge of duty on the soap supplied by a dealer in Maharashtra to a dealer in Karnataka, but the taxes on inputs used in producing the soap would be refunded to the dealer in Maharashtra by the Central and State tax authorities. This was found to be fraught with procedural difficulties of having a robust refund mechanism. Delay in granting refunds has been a common complaint made by trade and industry. It would also mean dealing with Central and State tax officials separately for obtaining the refunds of CGST and SGST duties.

The second model suggested zero rating of CGST but levying SGST equivalent to CGST and SGST rate which would be available as credit at the buyers end and would be levied and collected by State. For example, instead of the present IGST levied on interstate transfer which has to be collected by the Centre, the state would collect the interstate trade which would be an aggregate of Central and State taxes. This model did not find favour with the Centre as it saw this as an infringement of the Constitution.

The third model sought to impose an IGST integrated tax which would be the sum of CGST and SGST rates thus preventing arbitrage opportunities between inter-state and intra-state transaction and the IGST would be available as credit in the hands of the buyer. States here had some apprehensions about this being levied and collected by the Centre and saw in this move some erosion of their fiscal sovereignty. Initially it was visualised that the documents to facilitate availment credit on goods and services would be handled by the banking system. This again was found to be untenable as it was feared that this would burden the banking system. It could also impede the smooth flow of tax credit because of documentary delays. The seal of approval for the IGST model was finally given by the sub-committee set up by the Empowered Committee of State Finance Ministers in the 2012 Bhubaneswar session. The committee felt that IGST model would provide seamless credit at the front end even if it entails some problems of higher working capital requirements for trade and industry. The committee suggested that instead of the banking system the settlement of IGST credits between the Centre and the State could be done through the GSTN at the backend with seamless credit flow at the front end.

Cross Empowerment of Centre and State Tax Officials in Matters Relating to Compliance Verification

This issue proved to be most contentious and delayed the finalisation of the GST law. The crux of the administrative problem was the fear among Centre and State tax officials that their responsibility would be diluted and their administrative heft would come down post GST. Trade and industry also exerted pressure through their associations' indicating that they would find it difficult to deal with both Centre and State tax agencies together. They argued that there should be only dealing with only one agency as far as compliance verification was concerned which would include return scrutiny, audit and anti-evasion.

The threshold of ₹1.5 crore turnover became the key base negotiation position for the States. The reason for this threshold is because in the pre-GST scenario, there was an exemption on Central Excise Duty for goods up to a turnover of ₹1.5 crore. The state maintained that because the Centre in any case did not collect duty up to this turnover, the states should administratively deal with compliance verification of tax entity below this turnover. This view was predicated on the premise that Centre under its excise laws fully exempted goods up to an annual turnover of ₹1.5 crore. The Centre's counter argument was that for services their exemption limit was only up to ₹10 lakh. As goods and services together have to be considered the Centre argued that below ₹1.5 crore threshold limit for empowerment of States was not valid. After intense negotiation in the Council it was agreed that the units with the turnover of less than ₹1.5 crore would be subject to audit and return scrutiny by the States. This however marked the fact that the council had already agreed on the GST exemption for units up to annual turnover of ₹20 lakh and they had also agreed for a composition scheme for smaller units. This scheme provided for levy of flat rates of 1 per cent for traders and 2 per cent for manufacturers for annual turnover of up to ₹75 lakh. This arrangement effectively meant that both the Centre and State would not carry out any compliance verification of units with annual turnover up to ₹75 lakh except an online system scrutiny. The States would carry out return scrutiny and audit for units with turnover between ₹75 lakh to 1.5 crore. It was agreed that beyond ₹1.5 crore of annual turnover, both Centre and States would carry out compliance verification presumably on the basis of a shared list of units identified on the basis of risk parameters. The final solution did not completely please either the Centre or the States and probably the even distribution of displeasure facilitated a compromise around this arrangement.

These engaging debates really showed how reform works. What finally clinched the GST was really the perceived benefits from the GST. This was first the prospect of greater revenues due to reduction in non-compliance especially in the trading segment of the value chain. Second, was the expectation that the GST would boost domestic manufacturing through reduction in the incidence of duty, greater attractiveness of investment and an expanded domestic market. This point are further elaborated in the subsequent chapter. Finally, it ushers in digitisation in the tax process for ensuring that all tax entities would carry out key business processes online without physical interface with the tax administrator. It is for this reason that many tax experts felt that GST was an idea whose time had come to paraphrase Victor Hugo.

4

GST and Revenue Buoyancy

Revenue uncertainties have dominated discussions about the GST. This has been especially pronounced among the states which see the movement towards the GST as a leap in the dark.

What then are the reasons to assert that the implementation of GST will lead to revenue buoyancy? One can look for answers in the earlier experience of the states which implemented the VAT in 2004-05 when there was a similar air of 'revenue pessimism'. Table 4.1 indicates the trends in state VAT collections for the period 2001-02 to 2008-09 (covering both the pre-VAT and post-VAT periods).

Table 4.1

State Sales Tax Collection
(excluding CST, Petroleum, and Surcharge)

Year	*Revenue (₹ Crore)*	*Growth (%)*
2001-02	56,790	3.07
2002-03	66,748	17.50
2003-04	67,241	0.70
2004-05	89,609	33.30
2005-06	1,04,731	16.90
2006-07	1,28,775	23.00
2007-08	1,53,007	18.80
2008-09	1,78,715	16.80

Source: RBI reports.

One can see from the trends that 2004-05 (the year the state VAT was implemented) was an inflexion point when revenues went up sharply, indicating the impact of implementation of the state VAT that replaced the RST (retail sales tax). Even after the implementation of the VAT the revenue momentum was maintained. The revenue buoyancy could have been even more but for some states such as Tamil Nadu and Gujarat that retained generous sales tax deferral schemes. The debilitating effects of a conscious base erosion cannot be laid at the doorstep of the new tax. What is important is that this revenue buoyancy was achieved despite less than ideal design features of the state VAT: high thresholds, continuance of exemptions and a non-integrated IT system. It would therefore be fair to expect that the GST, with a far better design and a fully integrated IT system for both the Centre and the states, will deliver far greater revenue buoyancy.

The design of the GST suggests revenue buoyancy for other reasons. First, because of the phasing out of exemptions and the creation of an audit trail of transactions along the entire value chain, buyers will purchase goods and services only from a compliant supplier (to avail of full credit of taxes on input/intermediates). Second, as both the Centre and the states will tax concurrently a common taxable base, dual monitoring by both will improve compliance and boost revenues.

Third, services will bear a higher incidence of duty post GST, sharing a greater proportion of the tax burden—the rate effect. Fourth, as the taxable event in the GST shifts from 'manufacture' to 'supply of goods' more value addition in manufacturing will come into the tax net. Today, even though these are supposed to be covered under service tax, in practice they fall between the cracks in 'goods' and 'services'—the base effect will operate in manufacturing.

Finally, the GST Network that will provide the IT backbone for the tax has 'invoice-matching' features built into it. The application software developed by Infosys will match supplier information furnished in the return with the purchaser's details. Any mismatch not addressed within a stipulated time period will invite penal provision leading to denial of input credit. This will largely address the problem of input credit frauds.

While revenue buoyancy is assured by the very design of GST, there are some lost revenue opportunities and some lost tax credits embedded in capital goods due to the exclusion of real estate from the GST. There are huge advantages of including real estate in the GST, even more than the inclusion of alcohol and electricity. First, indirect tax collection data for 2014-15 indicates that the total amount of capital goods purchases on which CENVAT (central value-added tax) credit is availed of which about ₹1.60 lakh crore, divided between goods (₹1 lakh crore) and services (60,000 crore). National income account data suggest that investment in plant and equipment for 2014-15 by non-government and non-household units was about ₹7.5 lakh crore. Therefore, it would appear that the blocked taxes on capital goods could account for as much as 75 per cent of the total investment. A large portion of this investment is absorbed by the real estate sector. Inclusion of real estate in the GST would boost investment in the construction sector by bringing down capital cost and create jobs in what is probably the most employment-generating sector.

Second, it could be the third arrow in the quiver to battle the menace of black money income—the other two arrows being the recently passed Black Money (Undisclosed Foreign Income and Assets) and Imposition of Tax Act and the Benami Transactions Act. The GST could therefore be another instrument to fight black money income, and revenue gains could accrue by bringing more transactions in the open—the revenue gains could even be greater for direct taxes. The measure would clean up the land market, the most unreformed segment in the factor market reforms have largely focused on the product markets.

Sceptics must understand that transformational changes are not made by demonstrating caution. A good example is how Abraham Lincoln passed the Lands Grant Act, 1862, that provided land grants for setting up private universities (laying the base for the pre-eminence of American universities today) during the height of the Civil War when Confederate troops had almost reached the gates of Washington. The inclusion of real estate will be one such transformational move.

The very design of the GST will bring in revenue buoyancy, which can be cemented and secured by the inclusion of real estate. As the GST is being implemented when the economy is on an upswing, the revenue effect will be even more pronounced. Higher revenue generated can help create a strong safety net for the poor. Growth will promote welfare just as more welfare will make growth inclusive. Growth and welfare will then be the symbiotic twins they truly are.

The Constitution Amendment Act unifies the fractured value chain from raw material to retail by empowering Centre to tax value addition in trading and the States do levy tax on value addition in manufacturing and services. This has put in place a system of dual VAT in which the Centre and the States concurrently tax the entire value chain from raw material to retail. Hitherto, the Centre taxed the manufacturing part of the value chain whereas the States taxes the trading portion of the value chain as can be seen from Figure 4.1.

The pre-GST taxation system created disconnect between upstream and downstream value addition with adverse compliance consequences. It's important to understand this aspect in order to appreciate the significant revenue gains that are likely to accrue because of the GST. At present in the trading segment of the value chain, non-compliance is widely prevalent because traders do not get to avail any significant input duty credits as these are only confined to State VAT duties. By purchasing from VAT exempt traders a large portion of the trading community does business in the tax shadow region of the economy. In the GST regime, the situation changes dramatically as these traders now become eligible for tax credits on CGST duty paid on inputs goods, services and on capital goods and also on the IGST paid on imported goods. In case the trader does not declare his/her full value of transactions, he/she stands to lose out on these tax credits which will hang on him/her as costs and raise the prices. Therefore, the trader may declare volume of transactions just enough to offset the duty credits available to him/her in the earlier stages of the value chain. While there may not be any significant gains in GST revenues, they will show up in direct tax revenue because traders will pay higher corporate taxes on a higher reported GST turnover. Institutionally this is facilitated because the GST registration number which is a 15 digit number has embedded in it the 10 digit PAN code. It is therefore important to look at the revenue gains from direct taxes. In the medium term, GST revenues will also improve because of greater internal trade facilitated by removal of interstate barrier like the entry tax. Studies indicate that removal of non offsettable CST tax and the abolition of entry tax will expand the market by reducing the price of goods (lower pay-outs as costs and efficiency in the supply chain) and encourage manufacturing. The best example of this is the boom in demand for cars in the United States in the early part of the 20th century when Ford's T model based on assembly line production technique brought down prices significantly and made cars affordable to the aspirational middle class.

Figure 4.1

Value Chain Taxation: Central versus State

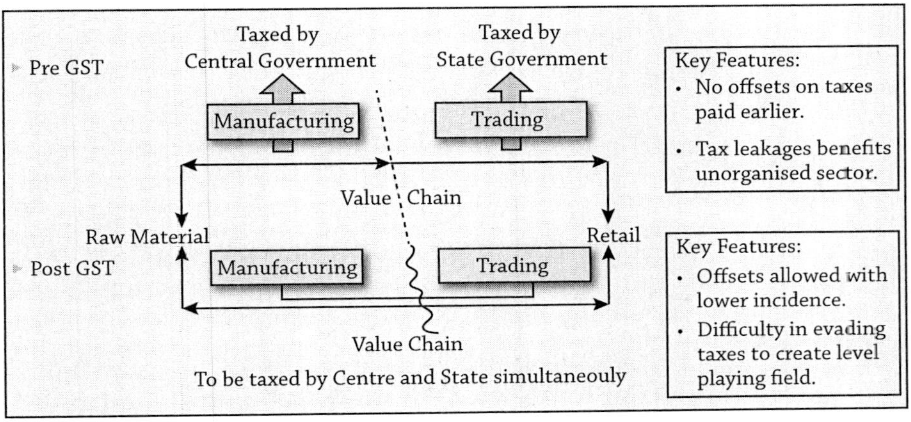

Fractured Value Chain for Taxation to be Unified under GST

To sum up, in the immediate short term, the revenue picture will be determined by whether revenue losses due to lowering of rates will be offset by better compliance. In the medium term, the expansion of the internal market and surge in manufacturing and services growth may create sustainable revenue growth.

5

GST: A Boost to Domestic Manufacturing

Indirect tax matters more to manufacturing than services because Central Excise taxation of Indian manufacturing, in a consolidated manner, came in 1944, 50 years earlier than in services. Traditionally manufacturing share in tax revenues has been higher than services—while constituting 18 per cent of GDP, the share of manufacturing in tax revenues has been around 80 per cent.

It is in this background that GST can make an important difference to the economic fortunes of manufacturing sector especially registered manufacturing. Why is this so? For this it is important to look at the GST impact both on the demand side and supply side factors. On the demand side the GST impact is likely to take three forms.

First, average tax incidence on manufacturing after taking into account all the subsumed taxes has come down. It is however difficult at this point of time to estimate the exact drop in tax incidence. However, evidence suggest that the drop is mainly due to reduction in the cascading effect of tax on tax which has happened because of subsuming of non-offsetable taxes like CST (central sales tax) and entry tax, and also because of new computation methods of levying CGST and SGST on the same basic price unlike earlier when State VAT was levied on a duty price inclusive of excise duty. Further, during the last three meeting of the GST Council ending on 6

October 2017, a large number of items have been shifted from the slot of 28 per cent to 18 per cent especially in major product categories like man made yarn, tractor components and pharmaceutical products. The drop in tax incidence on manufacturing can become significant going forward if the 28 per cent slot is abolished and the items in this category are transferred to the 18 per cent slot. A concept paper has recently been prepared and approved by the Council which lays down principle for shifting items from one duty slot to another instead of an ad hoc approach. Revenue loss due to this exercise could be reduced to some extent by increasing the duty on gold and gold jewellery from the present level of 3 per cent to 5 per cent and thereby also avoiding a special rate for this sector. Therefore, for all these reasons there could be a softening of prices of manufacturing products creating a demand expansion.

Second, domestic manufacturing also suffered from some negative protectionism at a macro level due to prevalence of a number of countervailing exemption which favoured imports. An estimate made in the Economic Survey 2017-18 showed that at an overall level the effective Central excise duty rate on manufacturing after taking into account exemptions was 9 per cent, but neutralisation through CVD (countervailing duty) exemption on imports was only 6 per cent; therefore the Indian industry faced negative protectionism of 3 percentage point. The GST has created a more level playing field for Indian manufacturing as most of the CVD exemptions have been phased away except for exporters importing duty free items. The IGST rate made applicable to imports would be the aggregate of CGST and SGST rates levied on similar items manufactured in India. Added to this is the additional mitigating factor that earlier the SAD (special additional duty) of 4 per cent did not neutralise the State VAT rate which varied from 5 per cent to 12 per cent. Therefore, this level playing field with imports will help to boost domestic manufacturing.

Third, the benefit of reduction in logistic cost is likely to accrue because of abolition of entry tax. Quicker movement of goods would facilitate maintenance of lower inventory level and abolition of CST could reduce the number of warehouses maintained by industry especially those catering to pan India markets like the FMCG sector. These state wise warehouses were maintained by various industry segments to avoid the payment of CST through effecting stock transfer of goods. This would become unnecessary in the GST regime as the CST stands abolished.

Finally, the big boost to manufacturing is likely to come from the expansion of a market created by abolition of entry tax leading to higher turnaround rate of commercial vehicles. Estimates made in the Economic Survey 2017-18 shows that cost of interstate trade are about 7 to 16 times higher than the cost of intra-state trade which is significantly higher than comparable standards for big federal countries like the USA and Brazil. GST would stimulate domestic manufacturing by opening up markets going beyond state boundaries. It is also likely that the sourcing of raw material would take place from newer locations in poorer eastern India which can emerge as new centres of growth. Domestic manufacturing can benefit from sourcing raw material/intermediates from cheaper sources hitherto disadvantaged by distance. Under GST, distance may not be dead but would certainly be diminished.

The supply side benefits in domestic manufacturing would mainly come from lowering of the cost of capital goods going into manufacturing because of unlocking of dead weight taxes. Prior to the GST implementation, State and Central taxes could not be offset because the Central taxes could not be offset against VAT and vice versa. First, with the integration of the value chain for the purpose of taxation from raw material to retail, seamless credit of duty would facilitate the transfer of tax incidence from intermediates and capital goods to final consumption. Second, GST is also likely to bring down the METR (marginal effective taxation rate) on a number of sectors because of unlocking of embedded taxes. This is explained in detail in the subsequent chapter 17.

In conclusion, both the demand side and supply side stimulation provided by GST will boost domestic manufacturing and will help 'Make in India' especially in the organised manufacturing sector.

6

GST and Ease of Doing Business

How GST Can Improve the Ease of Doing Business

The GST will also help industry by easing the cost of doing business. The information burden cast on industry today through multiple documentation and complexities is enormous. The business process re-engineering done in the GST will obviate the need for paper documentation by completely relying on online information furnished in the registration and returns module by the taxpayer.

The greatest advantage of GST for the manufacturer is harmonisation of the best business practices not only between the Centre and the states but among the states too.

Traditionally, indirect tax policymakers have accorded favourable tax treatment to the small and medium industry. This favourable treatment was provided on the premise that small-scale units use less amounts of capital per unit of output and also provide more employment per unit of output.

There is, however, not much evidence to establish that small-scale excise exemptions in the past have really helped in the growth of the small-scale sector.

Notwithstanding all this, the new GST law does protect the small-scale duty benefits. The GST Council, which is the joint policy formulating group consisting of both the Centre and the States, has accepted an annual threshold limit of ₹20 lakh turnover up to which GST will not be payable.

Beyond ₹20 lakh, for another additional ₹130 lakh annual turnover, the GST rates would be a flat 1 per cent for traders and 2 per cent for manufacturers based on self-certification of the turnover, or on the basis of the turnover declared in the financial accounts of the company.

Benefits

While the very small units are provided duty benefits or duty concessions, the GST does bring the small and medium units under a tight regulatory regime which would be IT-driven. Every unit paying GST must have a GSTN number after registration. Smaller units that are under the compounding scheme with a turnover between ₹20 lakh and ₹150 lakh would require to be registered with a GSTN number. There is now growing evidence that the small-scale exemptions in the past did not really incentivise the small-scale units to grow. On the other hand, they encouraged fragmentation in order to remain below the threshold level of exemption.

The big difference in GST is that the entire value chain, from raw material to retail, has become integrated for the purpose of taxation. The Constitutional Amendment Bill empowers the Centre to tax trading, and the States to tax services. The Constitutional Amendment really ushers in the dual VAT.

In the GST scenario, the decision to remain small would become counter-productive as units under-reporting transactions would suffer from blocked credits. Today, with the integration of the value chain for taxation, units would be eligible for credit for input goods, input services and imported capital goods. Many of them carry Central duties, which the State VAT-paying traders hitherto could not utilise.

Small businesses can build up a real time track record of tax payments digitally, and this can be used by lending institutions for credit rating and lending purposes. Currently, small businesses are credit-constrained because they cannot credibly demonstrate their financial capability.

We can, therefore, see in the GST scenario, more and more units in the informal sector pretending to be small, forced to enter the formal duty-paying segment. This would have significant revenue consequences, as it would also result in smaller units having to report higher incomes to the Direct Tax department in view of the synergy between Direct Tax and the Indirect Tax department established by the common PAN registration number.

It is also important to make a distinction between the small and medium industries in the goods sector and their counterparts in the services sector. The exemption threshold in the service sector was only ₹10 lakh compared to a turnover threshold of ₹1.5 crore on the goods side. Therefore, there has been less incentive to fragment and remain small in the services sector compared with the goods sector.

Compliance and After

The GST scheme announced by the Government spells out a clear design of the dual control regime.

This really covers the whole area of compliance verification.

Compliance verification has broadly three prongs, namely, return scrutiny, audit, and anti-evasion. It is now agreed that small units manufacturing goods below ₹1.50 crore annual turnover will have to deal locally with the State government. The small and medium units have, therefore, been protected from the vagaries of dealing with both the Central and the State indirect tax departments. This is undoubtedly a big relief.

Finally, where does all this leave the small and medium industry in the GST era?

The self-policing mechanism provided by the design of GST and the tracking of every transaction by the GSTN system will ensure a more level playing field for all units, whether big or small. The GST philosophy represents a shift in tax thinking, which is that tax incentives must be relied upon less and less to encourage particular segments of the industry. The tax rates must be low with fewer exemptions with a larger tax coverage of business entities.

Recent studies by the International Monetary Fund[1] and the World Bank have shown that tax incentives do not confer any real benefit but merely distort the resource allocation. Tax incentives introduce complexity into the tax system, because the rules themselves are complex and because tax authorities react to the tax planning that inevitably results from their introduction by putting into place anti-avoidance measures. This complexity imposes costs on administrators and taxpayers and increases the uncertainty of tax results. Uncertainty can deter the investment that the incentives are intended to attract. Small and medium units would be better off if there is greater ease of doing business which would require easing of the regulatory mechanisms, loosening of the labour laws, and greater access to bank credits. Expenditure switching from tax incentives to infrastructure spending could benefit small and medium units more than tax incentives. Perhaps this new thinking in the GST may end up helping the small and medium units even more.

There is a lot of disquiet about the large number of returns to be submitted under the GST. Even *The Economist* in a recent piece alluded to filing of 37 returns annually by a tax payer. The figure of 37 return is based on the three returns that everyone has to file every month in the form of GST 1, GST 2, GST 3 plus an annual return.

The filing of three returns together with an annual return has been one of the implementation challenges in the GST. Firms have found it difficult to generate the GSTR-2 which requires a system based validation of the invoices uploaded by the supplier by the buyer. In the GST Council meeting held on 4 May 2018, the whole issue of return filing was revisited. It was decided that there would be a three stage transition period culminating in the design of a single new return.

---

1. Source: Thuronyi, Victor (ed.) (1998). *Tax Law Design and Drafting*. Volume 2. International Monetary Fund.

In the first phase the present system of monthly filing of GSTR-3B (summary of output supplies and input supplies) and GSTR-1 (the list of outward supply invoices) for a B2B transaction would continue. This is appropriate as both these returns are well understood and are being increasingly filed with a fair degree of accuracy.

In stage two, GSTR-3B would continue and a new return design would also come into operation. Provisional credit would continue to be available during this stage through GSTR-3B. GSTR-1 would stand withdrawn in the second stage. Information in relation to credit on missing invoice and rejected invoice may be collected during this stage and an option created in law to impose a fees on availing provisional input tax credit on missing invoices. This option would be exercised, if the provisional credit does not come down over a period of time which is necessary for completing the transition.

In stage three, GSTR-3B would be withdrawn and also the facility for provisional credit would get withdrawn. The only return in operation thereafter would be the new return thus completing the transition. It is expected that stage two would not last for a period longer than six months. The details of the transition on above lines would be worked out in consultation with IT team and law committee.

The Council based on the reports from the Expert committee recognised that there was a need to move from a system based matching of input tax credit to a system of ensuring uploading of supply invoices through pressure exerted by the buyer. This was an important insight as it recognises that it is in the interest of buyers who avails input duty credit to ensure that the supplier uploads all his invoices based on the buyers own purchase register. This important change would mean that there would be no need for both the supplier and the purchase invoices to be uploaded and it would suffice if only the supplier invoices are uploaded. Therefore, going forward, there would be a movement towards a single return which would contain the outward supply invoices and the inward purchase invoices would be auto populated. Based on this the duty liability would be automatically system generated.

Therefore, in designing a single return the information to be contained in it would primarily be dictated by the need to automatically generate the monthly duty liability.

In view of the self-assessed nature of the return, the compliance verification both in the form of Return Scrutiny and Audit would be important. The approach in the GST system is to have a simple single monthly return and capture more detailed information required for compliance verification in the annual return. This would contain a lot of validated information from Form 3CD which assessee now submits to the Income Tax Department.

Finally, the Council also decided that it would be more prudent in view of the simplicity of the return to have the same periodicity of filing returns for both small and large taxpayers namely a monthly return. This would address the problem of large taxpayers reluctant to purchase from small taxpayers on account of delay in availing the input tax credit due to many small taxpayers opting for quarterly filing. Needless to mention in the case of quarterly filing, the final input credit picture emerges later leading to delay in the availment of input tax credit by the buyer. This would solve the problem of working capital blockages.

In conclusion, with the simplification of the return filing system, the advantages of the GST would be truly evident compared to the pre-GST system. The GST facilitates the ease of doing business by digitally aiding the taxpayers to complete the formalities for paying tax. The creation of an online portal in the GSTN will remove the physical interface between the tax payer and the tax administration, and create a tax friendly environment thereby also promoting the ease of doing business.

II
Implementation of GST

7

GST Implementation

Rates and Exemption Regime

The most audacious tax reform in post independent India was kicked off at a glittering midnight ceremony on 30 June/01 July 2017 in the historic central hall of the parliament. This was a reform long in its making but finally launched amidst considerably bonhomie among the Centre and the States. Implementation of the GST required a number of policy measures. Most important among them was the fitment of rates for the large number of commodities and finalisation of exemptions. It also required finalisation of key business rules relating to three business process namely registration, payment of duty, and submission of returns, which was to be handled centrally by an online portal created by the GSTN.

The Indian GST implemented with effect from 01 July 2017 is a dual GST in which the Centre and the States levy tax concurrently across the value chain. The existing indirect state taxes are subsumed in State GST, while the Central indirect taxes are subsumed in the Central GST. This is illustrated in the Figure 7.1.

IGST is levied on interstate transactions at a rate computed as the aggregate of CGST and SGST rates to avoid arbitrage between intrastate and interstate transactions.

Ideally, the GST should have included all goods and services in the taxable base. However to start with, alcohol, buildings and real estate, and electricity have been kept out of the GST. In the case of petroleum, the same has been brought within the GST but five products have been temporarily exempted from GST which includes crude oil, natural gas, petrol and diesel, and aviation turbine fuel which will be continue to be taxed under existing excise duties. This will provide some revenue comfort to the Centre and the States in the transition phase. The GST law provides that they can be brought back into the GST levy system when the GST council decides. There are two exclusions in the GST namely electricity and real estate.

Figure 7.1

Taxes Subsumed into GST

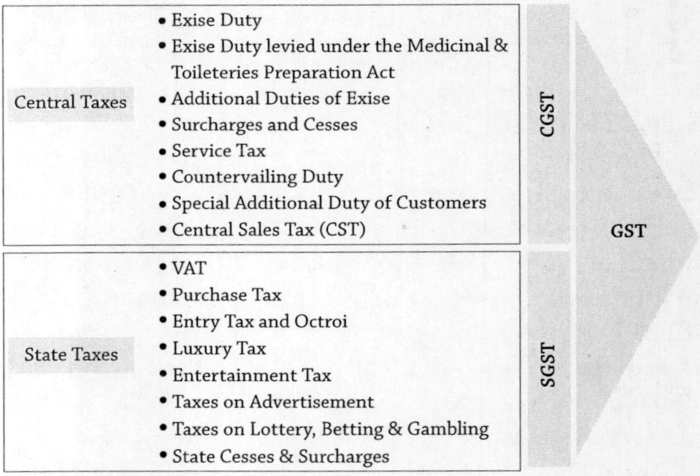

Source: Compiled by the author.

The GST council which is the main body vested with the task of deciding rates and exemption after lot of deliberations opted for a five tier rate structure—5 per cent, 12 per cent, 18 per cent, 28 per cent, 28 per cent *plus* Cess. It also approved a special 3 per cent rate for gold and gold jewellery. While deciding the fitment of various goods and services in the various rate slots, the GST council laid down the principle of equivalence. This meant that the technical team assisting the council would look at the existing rates of taxation by considering all the indirect tax rates applicable now, covering Central excise, service tax, VAT, entry tax, octroi, luxury tax, entertainment tax and purchase tax, then fit these items in the rate slot nearest to the prevalent aggregate duty rates. The rates of duties for some important items covering goods and services fixed by the GST council is given in Table 7.1.

Table 7.1

GST Rate for Goods and Services (Illustrative)

		Goods			
		Consumer	*Intermediate*	*Capital*	*Luxury/Sin*
Rate	0%	Poultry items (eggs, chicken), milk, curd, fresh fruits and vegetables, newspaper, contraceptives	Wheat, oil seeds, raw silk, salt, khadi yarn, jute fibres, flour	Electrical energy, wood fuel, handloom machinery	-
	5%	Skimmed milk, frozen vegetables, dry fruits, coffee, tea, vegetable oil, woven fabrics, PDS kerosene, LPG for household consumers, drugs or medicines including their salts	Vegetable fats, tobacco leaves, cocoa, mineral ores, gravel, insulin, building bricks	Machines for cleaning, sorting or grading seed, renewable energy devices & parts for their manufacture, rail locomotives, cargo ships	-
	12%	Apparel above ₹1000, frozen meat products, refined sugar, cell phones, diabetic food	Yarn of manmade fibres, granite blocks, wood pulp	Conveyor belts, hand pump, vacuum pump, harvesting or threshing machinery, tractors	-
	18%	Steel products, preserved vegetables, camera, tampons, biscuits, soap, insecticides	Software, wood tar, biodiesel, Iron and non-alloy steel, petroleum products (jelly, wax, etc.), bitumen	Aircraft engines, electrical transformers, tractor parts, printing machinery	
	28%	Chocolates, sunscreen, paint, washing machine, dishwasher, refrigerators	Molasses, granite, plywood, portland cement, glass	Fork-lift trucks, chassis fitted with engines, trailers	*Bidis*, pan masala, cigars, fireworks, aerated drinks, aircraft for personal use, luxury cars, lottery authorised by State governments

Rate	Illustrative List for Services		
	Producer Services	*Consumer Services*	*Government Services*
0%	Non-AC trains and buses, supply of farm labour, services relating to cultivation of plants and animal husbandry	Pilgrimage travel, hotels and lodges with tariff up to ₹1,000, healthcare, education, religious travel	Admission to "protected monuments", services provided by Reserve Bank of India, services provided by Fair Price Shops to CG
5%	Economy class travel in airlines, cab aggregators, transport of goods by rail, services of goods transport agency (GTA)	Services by way of housekeeping, such as plumbing, carpentering, Tour operator services	Railways
12%	Business class airline travel, transfer of IPR, construction services	Non-AC restaurants, hotel and lodges with tariff between ₹1,000 and ₹2,500	State run lotteries
18%	Financial services, IT, composite supply of works contract	Telecom, restaurants with AC and liquor license, hotels and tariff between ₹2,500 and ₹5,000	-
28%	-	Five star hotels and restaurants, cinema, gambling, horse race betting, services by way of admission to entertainment events	-

While the principle of equivalence was advanced to fix the rates, the question is whether the council had also some overreaching objectives in mind. The one objective which comes out very clearly is the goal of countering price rise. The intention was quiet clear that implementation of GST must not be seen as stoking inflationary fires. To understand this it would be useful to look at the weights of the various commodities in the CPI (consumer price index).

Figure 7.2

CPI: Various Commodities

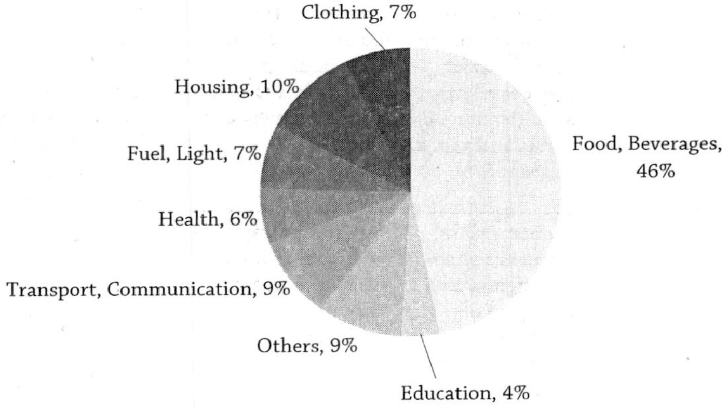

Source: GST Committee Report.

Figure 7.3

Share of Total Expenditure on Commodity for the Bottom 4 Deciles

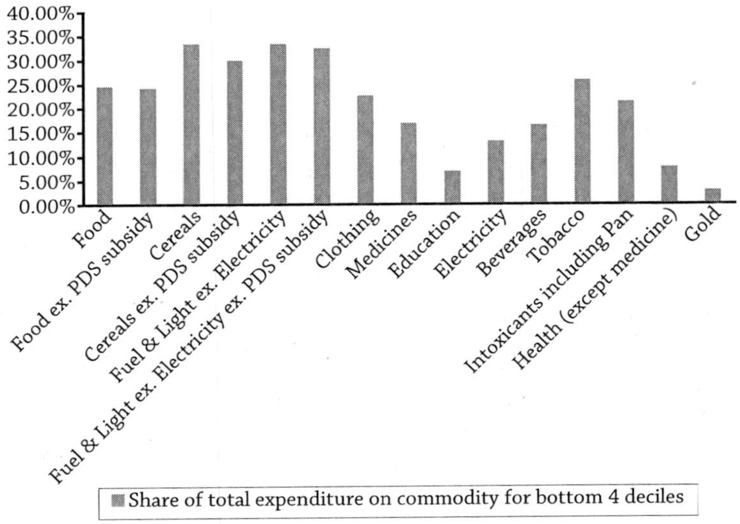

Source: GST Committee Report.

The rates approved by the GST council ensures that items with 60 per cent weight in CPI is kept exempted from GST levy while another 15 per cent is subject to levy of 5 per cent. This will ensure that the poorer sections would be protected from any increase in prices under GST. This conclusion is also strengthened if we look at the consumption pattern of the bottom four deciles of the populations.

The other important objective which the council had in mind was to encourage sectors which are labour intensive. This was probably inevitable given the current concerns on the job front. Recent econometrics evidence suggests that employment elasticity of industrial growth is declining. Two sectors which fit this categorisation are textiles and food processing.

Textiles is probably one of the most employment intensive industry in India employing a large number of artisans and weavers. India has a rich tradition of weaving skills in all parts of the country. In the textile sector, the GST council has got many things right but some wrong. The council has fixed a uniform rate of 5 per cent on cotton yarn and fabrics and apparel of value less than ₹1,000. It has also fixed a 5 per cent rate on job work services like stitching, weaving, etc. in relation to textiles. This is welcome as a large number of tasks in the textile industry are outsourced to workers in small establishments outside the discipline of registration. Some calculation shows that the effective incidence of duties on these segments will come down from 8-9 per cent currently to 5 per cent if we consider all the existing duties leviable namely central excise, state VAT, octroi entry tax and purchase tax. GST certainly will therefore give a fillip to the textile industry. The critical change that will happen is that fabrics which were outside the ambit of duty in the value chain will now become part of the duty regime which will considerably reduce non-compliance and link the fabric to the apparels in the duty chain. The latter will benefit from getting credit of duty on fabric. This will send a comforting message to the compliant assesses. The duty on man-made fibre and yarn initially put at 18 per cent GST rate was brought down to 12 per cent by the GST council at its meeting on 6 October 2017. Even this could further be brought down to 5 per cent making the tax rate uniform across the value chain. The report of the textile industry prepared by the Chief Economic Advisor suggested fibre neutrality in taxation. This opinion was predicated on the argument that world trade is now moving towards synthetics. Even for domestic purposes given the climate conditions many Textile Committees have suggested use of blends of cotton and synthetics—combining the comfort of cotton with the durability of synthetics.

The decision to have differential rate of duties between apparels of a value less than ₹1,000 (5%) and those above ₹1,000 (12%) also deserves review at some stage. The rich-poor argument which may appear attractive on the surface masks the important fact that many products consumed by the rich are produced by the poor. Therefore, in trying to tax the consumption of the rich the higher tax levy may actually hit the poor. It would have been therefore far better if a uniform rate of 5 per cent had been fixed for the entire textile industry across the value chain irrespective of the nature of the activity and the nature of the fibre. This was important because a great policy opportunity now presents itself to take the textile industry to great heights and provide gainful employment to the large number of weavers and artisans. Historically, the textile industry is a good example of how wrong policies adversely affected the growth of the sector. At the time of independence, the textile industry was poised to become the leader in Asia but high rates of import duty on textile machinery and a policy of reserving textile items for the small scale industry effectively prevented the emergence of large textile companies in the 1970s; the space was taken over by China, Taiwan and South Korea. Today another opportunity presents itself provided we simplify and lower the rates especially on synthetics and maintain fibre neutrality in taxation.

Substantial reduction in duty has been provided to processed foods. The duty rates in these segments will be coming down from the present level of 26-28 per cent to 12 per cent. This has been done because government realises the strong employment potential of this sector. While India processes roughly 10 per cent of its horticulture products, even countries like Brazil process 75 per cent of their production. Manufacture of processed food with higher value addition can enhance farmer incomes. In times of agrarian distress this would be an appropriate policy response. With the government seriously considering allowing foreign direct investment in the food processing segment, this rate reduction will certainly create a favourable ecosystem.

Tobacco

A very interesting rate decision is the imposition of 5 per cent GST on unmanufactured tobacco in the hands of the purchaser. This is an important measure as it recognises that from the health point of view, all tobacco needs to be treated uniformly for tax purposes without discriminating between product categories. The measure will also bring in discipline in the tobacco auction markets and create an audit trail of transactions which will reduce non-compliance in sectors such *bidi*, chewing tobacco and cigarettes. It may also bring in much needed revenue to the extent tobacco finds use in the exempted product categories.

Works Contract

The other interesting decision was fixing a duty rate of 12 per cent for works contract relating to construction of residential/commercial buildings where the full value of the land is included in the taxable base. Full input duty credit has been allowed whereas hitherto no credit was given on input goods. This measure could be the precursor to the inclusion of real estate and buildings in the GST in the next around. This will bring the full value chain in the real estate segment within the GST which until now is confined only to the construction stage. It will remove the present artificial distinction in services taxation between work contracts and services rendered in relation to construction of residential/commercial buildings. This will help clean up the land market and reduce the generation of black money income by bringing in greater transparency in transactions.

Gold and Jewellery

The fixation of rate of duties on gold and gold jewellery was a contentious issue and was vigorously debated in the GST council. The council finally decided on the rate of 3 per cent going marginally above 2 per cent prevalent now (1% excise and 1% VAT). Contrary to conventional wisdom the pattern of gold and gold jewellery ownership is heavily skewed. This is shown in Table 7.2.

Table 7.2

Decile-wise Share in Gold Consumption

Decile (Top to bottom)	*Percentage Share in Gold Consumption*	*Cumulative Share*
1	63.4	63.4
2	16.4	79.7
3	6.9	86.6
4	4.5	91.1
5	3.4	94.5
6	2.6	97.1
7	1.3	98.4
8	0.9	99.4
9	0.4	99.8
10	0.2	100.0

Source: NSS data and GST committee calculations.

Table 7.2 shows clearly that the top two deciles of the population categorised by income, account for nearly 80 per cent of the consumption of gold. Therefore, clearly increase in the duty rates for gold and gold jewellery would fall on the well to do sections of society. The council could have opted for a higher rate of 5 per cent which would have provided additional revenue cushion to bring more consumer items currently fixed under 28 per cent bracket into the 18 per cent bracket. For example, there is no reason why washing soaps is at 18 per cent and washing powder is at 28 per cent. This could have helped to slowly bring the 28 per cent category items into the 18 per cent category. This would have helped to reduce the duty rates on a large number of consumer items, expanding the market and bringing these products within the reach of the growing aspirational middle class.

The counter argument that higher duty rates would encourage smuggling appeared to have carried the day. However, CBIC data which was presented in the GST report does not bear this out. Figure 7.4 indicates that increase in import duty rate of gold in the past did not lead to rampant increase in smuggling.

Figure 7.4

Gold Imports in India

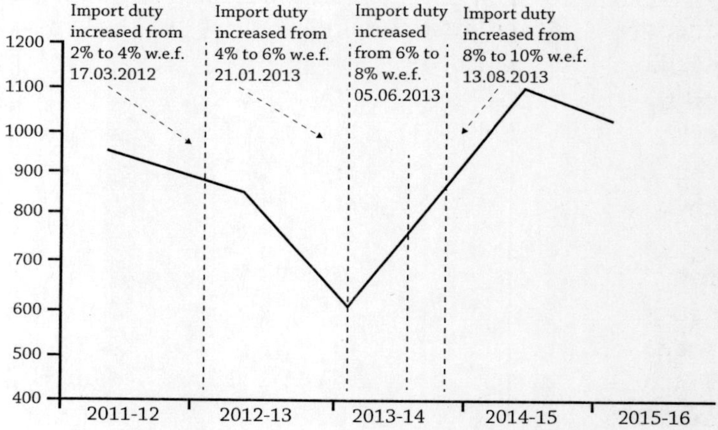

Source: CBIC.

Domestic prices of gold are a function of the level of international prices abroad and inflationary expectations at home. On the international side, gold has ceased to be an attractive store of value given the emergence of new financial instruments such as digital bitcoins and low levels of inflation. The relative strengthening of the US dollar makes gold even less attractive. The Government's Jan Dhan Yojana has given the poor greater access to credit, and their financial inclusion will make gold less attractive.

Exemptions

Exemptions conceptually have no place in the GST system. This is because they create blockages in the free flow of credit in a multi stage taxation system. The large number of exemption given today is the main reason why it is difficult to compute the effective incidence of taxation on any product.

For example, today tractors are exempt from central excise duty but the effective incidence of tax on tractors is around 12 per cent on account of the embedded taxes on the inputs used in making tractors. The non-offsetability of input taxes arises because of exemptions on the final product. Therefore, from a policy maker's point of view, phasing of exemption provides transparency on the effective incidence of duty on the final product. Therefore, when exemptions are phased out, a zero per cent duty on tractors in the pre-GST period is actually equivalent to 12 per cent duty in the post-GST system. Having said this, it may not be possible for government to phase away all exemptions. Today the States give exemptions to 90 products whereas the Centre exempts 300 products. In the discussions with the States, there was a general consensus that the Centre should exempt only those products which are also exempted by the State. This would result in the phasing away of a number of central exemptions.

The list of GST exemptions given in respect of goods is placed at Annexure 1. As stated above, these exemptions broadly cover VAT exemptions given by the State. These cover essential food products such as milk, vegetables, salt, fresh fruits, egg, meat and flour. Items like jute and newspapers are also exempted. In the services sector, the exemptions broadly cover education and healthcare services, services provided by government and public sector agencies and also services covering sovereign functions of the government. List of these exemptions are detailed at Annexure 2. The IGST exemptions cover those items where there is no manufacturing activity in India, for example: IGST exemption is given for import of aircrafts into India. Also, certain imports made by research institutions are exempted. A list of such IGST exemptions in placed at Annexure 3.

The GST has also provided an opportunity to phase out a large number of CVD and SAD exemptions. Their duties were levied to neutralise the disadvantages faced by the domestic producers who were paying central excise duty and state VAT respectively. The phasing away of these exemptions would remove the negative protectionism faced by the domestic manufacturers vis-á-vis imports. This will give a boost to domestic manufacturing in India. Taxpayers/manufacturers must be educated on the disadvantage of having exemptions. To many, this may not be obvious because what taxpayers see are only the visible output taxes and not the actual effective incidence of tax after taking into account the embedded taxes. There is also now growing evidence on the basis of studies done by World Bank and IMF that tax exemptions do not help but only hurt industry. Their effectiveness has been contested and the consensus is that tax incentives work only when they are targeted properly. For example, tax incentives given for research and development sometimes do work. In many cases it was found that tax incentives are given to industries who in any case may have attracted investments even without tax incentives. This is because investors are also guided by considerations other than tax. This would include factors like labour cost, depth of the market, institutional and regulatory arrangements and effective enforcement of contracts. The GST's great achievement may therefore lie not only in 'banishing the inspector *raj*' but the 'exemption *raj*' as well.

In conclusion, the rates and exemption regimes finalised by the GST council are a huge improvement on the pre-GST system. Overall, there is likely to be a reduction in the incidence of duty on most products. This will definitely help organised manufacturing which will be the biggest beneficiary of the GST implementation.

8

GST and Compliance Verification

All tax reforms can be viewed through the prism of how it impacts key business processes. These are: 'registration', 'payment of duties (including refund)', 'submission of returns', 'return scrutiny', 'audit', 'anti-evasion' and 'dispute resolution'.

In the GST scheme three processes—'registration', 'payment of duty' and 'submission of returns'—representing the assessment function is being handled separately by the GSTN portal. Therefore, the Centre and the State tax departments will have a limited role in this area except to periodically review the business rules. The existing rules represent the agreement reached by the Centre with the State tax administrations. They are detailed and may not interest the lay reader. Therefore, these are annexed as chapter references.

The other business process namely—'return scrutiny', 'audit' and 'anti-evasion'—representing the compliance verification function will be administered by both Central and State tax officials through their tax administrations. Fortunately, the CBIC built up a strong compliance verification system through two important capacity development projects: one to develop a strong Audit Manual with assistance from the Canadian Development Agency between 1996 and 2004 and the other with the Asian Development Bank between 2006 and 2010 to replicate the same for 'return scrutiny'. The strengthening of the compliance verification system within the CBIC is an interesting story to recount for it holds lessons going forward into the GST.

The compliance verification story really began in the early 1990s, when in 1994 the CBIC introduced an invoice based assessment as a precursor to implementing the Central VAT. In this system, the transaction value declared by the assesse in the invoice was accepted as the taxable value except in situations where prices were not the sole consideration of the sale. This was followed by the introduction of self-assessment system in 1995-96, when assessment functions were transferred from the tax officers to the tax assesse who was legally empowered to determine his/her duty liability. This was a radical development in the tax department for the system reposed trust in the assesse. Around the same period in 1995-96, Dr Manmohan Singh, the then Finance Minister, visited Canada. During his visit, he was greatly impressed by the professionalism of the Canadian Audit system. Discussions with Canadian counterpart led to the signing of a Capacity Development Agreement between the Finance Ministry and the Canadian Revenue Department (later converted into the Canadian Revenue Agency). This project sought to create a strong audit programme which could help improve compliance without being administratively intrusive and was funded by the Canadian International Development Agency (CIDA).

A large number of Revenue Department officers from CBIC visited Canada and got closely acquainted with the audit procedures. Senior Canadian officers also visited India during the same time. These visits led to adoption of an audit methodology which later led to the preparation of the Audit Manual. The whole audit programme was called 'Excise Audit 2000', for it was implemented from 1 April 2000. One Canadian-officer who played a very important role was a Canadian Indian officer named Girish Shah. He interacted closely with the National Training Academy to train the trainers and also played a very important role in drafting the Audit manual. The important steps in the audit methodology which emerged as a result of the project are attached at the end of the chapter. The seven steps in the audit methodology was popularised as '*shaadi ke saat phere*' just to emphasise the sacrosanct nature of the audit methodology. The new audit methodology replaced the earlier routine scrutiny of returns. As is natural in any change, there was initial resistance from some senior officers for the new system required their greater involvement going beyond an earlier managerial role. The new audit project was disparagingly dubbed as 'KIDA Audit' a play on the 'CIDA Audit' (funding being provided by the Canadian Development agency). But this was not so much opposition as a fear of the unknown.

The introduction of the audit methodology was complemented by one the most comprehensive training programme undertaken by the CBIC. Between 2000 and 2010, all the officers and the staff were trained in the scrutiny of financial records. Without improvement in the financial literacy the audit project could not have been successful. Noteworthy was the exemplary leadership provided by R.K. Chakraborty who headed the project during its entire span and retired as Member CBIC. He had the uncanny knack for discovering young talented officers across the country who cut their teeth in the project. Many of them later flowered in their careers. This approach of R.K. Chakraborty reminded us of what the late L.K. Jha said to one of the senior officers when asked about the secret of his success: "I have always sought and benefited from the company of the young".

The training drive was particularly important because while world over tax administrations used professional auditors to audit, the CBIC sought to reinvent its own officers as auditors, especially those who had a background in accountancy and proficiency in the use of computers. This approach was immediately reflected in a dramatic improvement in audit outcomes which is reflected in Table 8.1.

Table 8.1

A. EA2000 Audits (New Methodology)

S. No.	*Year*	*No. of Audits*	*Total Detection (INR in Crore)*	*Total Spot Recovery (INR in Crore)*	*Detection Per Audit (INR in Lakh)*	*Recovery Per Audit (INR in Lakh)*
1	2000-01	1441	647	47	44.89	3.42
2	2001-02	4183	1277	76	30.52	1.81

B. Other Audits (Old Methodology)

S. No.	*Year*	*No. of Units Audits*	*Total Short Levy Detected (INR in Crore)*	*Total Spot Recovery (INR in Crore)*	*Detection Per Audit (INR in Lakh)*	*Recovery Per Audit (INR in Lakh)*
1	2000-01	24528	362	31	1.48	0.13
2	2001-02	16524	332	27	2.01	0.16

Note: As both audits were carried out side, by side a comparative assessment was possible. From 2002-03 onwards all audits were based on the new methodology.

Source: DG Audit, CBIC.

Table 8.1 shows the priority of audits shifted from quantum to quality of audits and the audit recoveries dramatically improved. A number of new ideas were also thrown up during the project period, especially the use of risk management techniques and computer assisted audits. The Indian revenue officers were able to borrow an interesting software called 'WINIDEA' which was used to audit the records of large companies. In the absence of this system, manual audit would have required considerable time and resources. Three centres were first built up in Indore, Pune, and Bangalore, mainly because some of the officers trained in these techniques were located at these places and skills were later disseminated to other centres. The CBIC today has an Audit Manual both for services and goods. It has a Risk Management Manual and an Audit Training Manual. The methodology adopted is independent of the law and therefore can be easily used in the GST scenario. The Centre and the States can now collaborate on preparing a common GST Audit Manual.

In addition to the improvement of the audit system, the 'CIDA project' also prodded the CBIC to look at the automation of its business processes. A cerebral Canadian officer 'Mr Landsberg' came to India and met a number of officers especially from the Directorate of Systems. His important message was "you can't automate unless you review and revisit your business processes for redundancy and ineffectiveness." Business process reengineering became thereafter a buzzword in the Department. This message was conveyed through pithy slogans like: "Don't pave the cow path" and "Don't try to put lipstick on a frog". The underlying message was that business process reengineering must precede computerisation. The Canadian project ended in 2005-06, but not before it had created a huge impact on the audit system in the CBIC. Audit based control was internalised by the officers of the department as a result of this project which was also complemented by a very crucial skilling programme in the scrutiny of financial records.

As the audit project ended and the CIDA commitment ended, the Finance Ministry also realised the importance of strengthening the 'return scrutiny' system on similar lines. Dr Vijay Kelkar who was in the finance ministry at that time persuaded the Asian Development Bank (ADB) to continue the capacity development project with the Canadian Revenue Agency. The importance of the return scrutiny was emphasised by the report of the Task Force of the Indirect Tax in 2002 prepared under his Chairmanship. His observations really provided guidance for the preparation of the Return Scrutiny Manual:

> It is our view that assessment should be the primary function of the Central Excise officers. Self-assessment on the part of the tax payer is only a facility and cannot and must not be treated as a dilution of the statutory responsibility of the Central Excise officers in ensuring correctness of duty payment. There is no doubt that Audit and Anti-evasion have their roles to play, but assessment or confirmation of assessment should remain the primary responsibility of the Central Excise officers.

The Manual for Return Scrutiny prepared under the ADB project was visualised as an add-on to the online scrutiny mainly to evaluate the correctness of assessment. This was especially important for carrying out compliance verification of smaller units who were large in number and were not generally audited. The main guidelines for return scrutiny are also attached at the end. Unlike the audit project the return scrutiny programme has still not gained traction. One of the reasons could be that at the field formation level there is a lack of clarity on the role of audits vis-á-vis return scrutiny. Going forward there is the prospect of greater success in view of the information sharing MoU signed between CBIC and CBDT in November 2014. Information relating to TDS has proved to be useful in detecting non-compliance especially in the area of service tax during return scrutiny. This information available in Form 26 AS provides the tax deduction which is normally a percentage of the taxable turnover. From the rate applied for a particular service, automatically the value of the taxable service reported can be deduced and this can be compared with the turnover reported in the GST return now. As the section under which the TDS deduction is made is also indicated in the Form 26AS statement, the nomenclature of relevant taxable service can be deduced.

The return scrutiny system would also require a robust risk assessment system which can select delinquent units from a large number of small taxpayers. In a sense therefore, both audit and return scrutiny can complement each other by focusing on the compliance verification of large and small tax payers respectively.

The compliance verification story really has an important lesson going forward. The Centre and the State Tax Departments need to come together and collaborate for preparation of a standard Audit and Return Scrutiny Manual. This is likely to be the big project in the coming days. Past experience shows that leadership and skilling are important attributes for the success of a project. The State can learn from the CBIC experience and build upon the manuals already prepared. Success will come only when we seek not shun new ideas.

Guidelines for Return Scrutiny

The return scrutiny programme implemented by the CBIC which was contained in the return scrutiny manual visualised a two stage scrutiny system namely, a) online scrutiny of all returns filed; b) detailed manual scrutiny for ensuring correctness for selected returns of an assesse, identified on the basis of risk parameters. By its very nature, online and detailed scrutiny have different objectives and different sample segments. The purpose of online scrutiny is the following:

- Completeness of the information furnished.
- Description of the unit including assignment of HSN code and the registration details.
- Timely filing of returns.
- Timely payment of duties.
- Identification of the non-filers and stop filers.

The detailed scrutiny as explained above is to ensure correctness of assessment in respect of few selected units identified on the basis of risk parameters. The detailed scrutiny programme would also serve as a work load development programme by initiating a referral programme for audit and anti-evasion.

The GST law empowers the GST officers to take up the return scrutiny. These provisions are contained in Section-59, GST Law, Scrutiny of Returns. The feature of the provisions are:

(a) the proper officer may scrutinise the return and related particulars furnished by the taxable person to verify the correctness of the return in such manner as may be prescribed;

(b) the proper officer should inform the taxable person of the discrepancies noticed, if any, after such scrutiny in such manner as may be prescribed and seek his explanation thereto;

(c) in case the explanation is found acceptable, the taxable person shall be informed accordingly and no further action should be taken in this regard; and

(d) in case no satisfactory explanation is furnished within a period of 30 days of being informed by the proper officer or such further period as may be permitted by him/her or where the taxable person, after accepting the discrepancies, fails to take the corrective measure in his return for the month in which the discrepancy is accepted, the proper officer may initiate appropriate action.

With reference to correctness in the return, the GST legislation has to be read as correctness of the assessment. This correctness of assessment cannot be done through online scrutiny and therefore requires a limited manual scrutiny programme linked to robust risk management system which can correctly identify the delinquent units. Rules also provides for Government to formulate guidelines for scrutiny of the returns. The existing manuals could be used as a basis to prepare the GST manuals. Typically the detailed manual scrutiny programme can do the following:

(i) match the taxable turnover in the tax return with the audited company return submitted to the Income Tax department;

(ii) match the export turnover in the return with the turnover reported in the profit & loss account;

(iii) broadly look at correlation between inputs used and output outcomes;

(iv) evaluate in the case of services the appropriateness of the duty rate applied in the case of mixed and composite supply; and

(v) evaluate the correctness of the open market value in the case of business to customer transaction;

To summarise, the return scrutiny programme is a core function of the tax department. It has to be supported by a good risk management system.

Guidelines for Audit

Audit Process

The seven steps of Audit 2000:

1. Selection of the unit
2. Desk review
3. Gathering and documenting systems information
4. Evaluation of internal control
5. Preparation of audit plan
6. Conduct of audit according to the audit plan
7. Post audit monitoring

Step 1

The Planning Cell's must provide information about the past compliance record of the company and also provide updated details about the assessee master along with the copy of the trial balance obtained from the assessee.

The DG Audit has circulated risk scores for all units with an annual duty payment of ₹10 lakh a month which may be used for selection.

Selection of the units must be done by JC/ADC in consultation with Commissioner.

Selection may also require identification of any particular area or product segment of the company for compliance verification.

After selection, an intimation letter in a prescribed format must be sent giving an audit notice of atleast 15 days.

Step 2

The most important feature of this step is reconciliation of the information given in the financial records with the information submitted in the return (reconciliation must be done for the year as a whole).

The following areas of reconciliation are required common for both goods and services which are in the nature of a risk loss analysis.

Reconciliation of the taxable turnover reported in the returns with the estimated turnover derived from the trial balance (risk loss of duty)

Reconciliation of the input tax credit availed in the return with the input tax availment derived from the purchase of inputs given in the purchase account in the trial balance (risk loss of credit)

Annual Abstract Statement of Goods Manufactured/Traded-Product Wise

Subject	*Quality*	*Value*	*Remarks*
Opening Balance			
Production/Clearances			
Closing Balance			

Estimation of transaction value from the annual abstract statement in the production ledger

Production Cost = Opening Balance + Production – Closing Balance
Cost of Sales = Production Cost + Profit + Selling Costs
Transaction Value = Cost of Sales/Quantity Cleared

Step 3

Gathering and Documenting Systems Information

Through Interview

↓

Main focus is in Interview

↓

- Queries could be the following (indicative list):
- Purchase system
- Sales system
- Inventory system
- Important events in the unit
- New products introduced
- Whether services are provided (can be correlated from expenditure account)
- Details of quality certification

Through Tour of the Plant for goods

↓

Ascertain whether job work is done for other manufacturers or services are provided to other manufacturers/service receipt

Step 4

Evaluation of Internal Control

Validate the responses given during the interview through walk through of samples invoices of important inputs, capital goods and important final products.

⬇

Typically validate the responses given to functioning of the main line systems like purchase, sales and inventory systems and then evaluate the risk.

⬇

Do a walkthrough of a sample return in conjunction with an officer from the company who has prepared the return—this will give the audit officer an insight into the financial records of the company—the AC leading the team must do this and document the same in the working papers.

Step 5

Preparation of the Audit Plan

Preparation of the audit plan would be based on the points which have emerged with a bearing to non-compliance in earlier steps 1 to 4 and the process of enquiry and responses must be documented in the working papers.

The various entries in the audit plan format must be spelt out—process/instruments should not be with the subjects taken up for audit.

Four Subjects can be:

- Dutiability.
- Classification.
- Valuation.
- Input tax Credit.

Illustrative example of a model Audit Plan

Subject	*Specific Issue*	*Field Document*	*Source Document*	*Selection Criteria*	*Remarks*
Valuation of Final Products Services	Inclusion of testing charges in the transaction value of batteries	Product Service	Testing charges account in the Trial Balance	Invoices ending with SI No.5 in the month	Sample invoices of those months may be taken when maximum sales of batteries has taken place

Step 6

Conduct of Audit according to the Audit Plan

Study the documents identified in the audit plan to determine whether non-compliance is established.

The verification papers must document the duty non-compliance through reference to documents and cite the relevant provisions of the Law which have been transgressed.

Quantification of the demand must be done.

Matter could be discussed either by the AC or DC with the senior management for voluntary compliance of the audit demands.

Suggestion for improvment of the Internal Control System of the company could also be included in the verification papers and shared with the management of the company.

Step 7

Post Audit Monitoring

The audit paras raised must be discussed in the monthly EMC meeting which would be chaired by the Commissioner.

↓

The concerned audit team and the range officers/AC must be present to explain the non-compliance.

↓

SCN must be prepared and issued by the audit party.

↓

ADG (Audit's) representatives may also attend the meeting—the copy of the working papers may be shared with ADG (Audit).

↓

Voluntary compliance points may be discussed separately to decide whether request for waiver of SCN and penalty is to be considered.

9

GSTN for Implementation of GST

It would be no exaggeration to say that the GSTN is the key to GST. The importance of creating a strong technological backbone for implementation of GST was first visualised by the Empowered Committee of Finance Ministers when the first discussion paper on GST was released in November 2009. Following upon on this, in July 2010, the Finance Ministry setup an Empowered Group for development of an IT system required for GST regime under the chairmanship of Nandan Nilekani. Between 2010 and April 2012, widespread consultation took place on the architecture of the GSTN. One view was that the GSTN should be housed within the Government while the other view was that it should be setup as a SPV (special purpose vehicle) outside the government with majority private participants. As in the case of Aadhar, out of the box thinking prevailed. In April 2012, GSTN as a SPV was approved for creation by the Government. The structure visualised was as follows:

Incorporated on 28th March 2013:

- Under Section 25 of the Companies Act, 1956.
- As a private limited company.

Promoted jointly by the Central and State governments with the following equity structure:

- Central government: 24.5 per cent.
- EC & State government: 24.5 per cent.
- Private financial institution: 51 per cent.

The Nandan Nilekani committee opined that having majority private sector participation in the GSTN would facilitate faster decision making, unencumbered by detailed government procedures and would facilitate induction of the best talent by paying market salaries. The architecture visualised was a common GST portal with the following features:

1. Common PAN based registration.
2. Common standardised return for all taxes (with different account heads for CGST, SGST and IGST).
3. Common standardised challan for all taxes (with different account heads for CGST, SGST and IGST).

The diagrammatical depiction is given below:

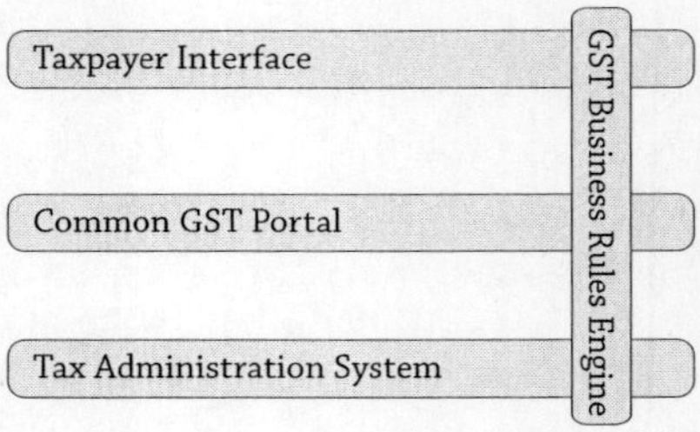

The audacious idea that the Committee came up with was to look at invoice matching overriding the diffidence of the tax authorities. Here, Nilekani's key insight was that capturing invoice level information can be translated into invoice level matching for business to business transactions. This was aided by the refund technological advance in storage and processing capabilities. It was felt that the GSTN besides collecting tax revenue could also be used as a powerful instrument to prevent revenue leakages. The committee also suggested that initially the GSTN could focus on centralising and taking ownership of three key business process namely registration, payment of duty, and submission of return. In case of other business process like compliance verification and dispute resolution, the Centre and the States could opt for doing it themselves or delegating it depending on their technical capabilities.

The GSTN that has been implemented today owes a lot to the vision of Nandan Nilekani and his team who were able to look ahead and visualise a world class IT system. The scheme of handling the key business processes through a common portal and the tax data transfer to the various stakeholders is shown below:

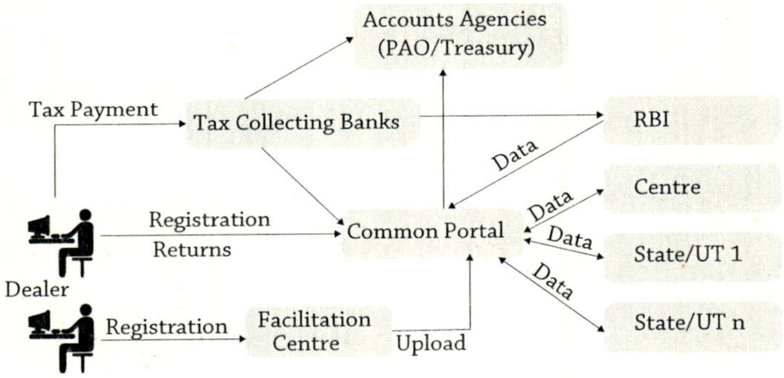

The common GST portal created and managed by GSTN will also do this matching on the basis of invoice level data filed as part of the return by all taxpayers. Similar exercise will be done for dealer

Interstate supplies where goods or services move from the state of origin to the state of consumption along with the tax payments, the claim of IGST and its utilisation is settled based on returns filed at the common GST portal. GSTN will create and maintain the information on IGST based on return of taxpayers. This data will be used for settlement of funds between Centre and States.

For the smooth roll-out of the GSTN in the first phase, the three core processes of registration, payment and submission of returns have been operationalised and made available to all the 80 million taxpayers. Under the scheme visualised for registration, the migration of existing taxpayers to the new system leads, to allotment of the GST registration number (GSTIN) which is a 15 digit PAN based identification number. Needless to mention, nobody with turnover above the GST threshold, can carry out business in a post GST era without a GSTIN. The new entities need to apply for fresh registrations and obtain their GSTIN. Every registrant after the validation of the PAN number with the income tax database is assigned online a GSTIN, a user ID and a password. This allows the taxpayers to use the GSTIN system.

The first implementation of the GSTN is depicted below:

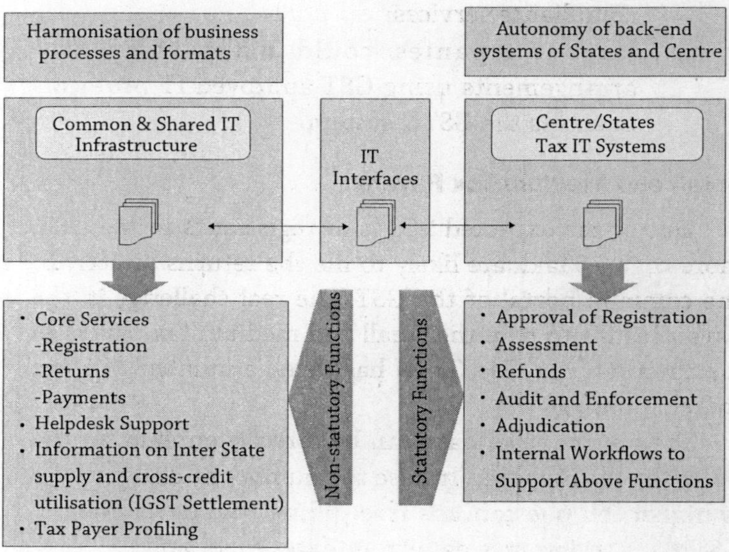

The scheme for submission of returns requires all returns to be submitted to the GSTN system. A common return format is prescribed for tax payers all over India. As part of the return filing process, taxpayers would need to reconcile their purchase transaction with those reported by their vendors to be able to avail input tax credit. GSTN will facilitate this by automatically creating purchase registers for taxpayers based on supply transactions reported by their vendors.

The duty payment system through the GSTN visualises payment of GST through a variety of modes such as internet banking and credit/debit card, OTC (over the counter) payment and payment made through RTGS/NEFT from other banks. This requires integration of the GST system with various agency banks for internet payments and multiple gateway operators for card payments.

The tax payers can interact with the GSTN system in three following ways:

(a) direct access to the website of GSTN;
(b) access through GST Suvidha Providers (GSPs) who in turn uses secured channel to access the

GSTN system—these GSPs are expected to provide value added services apart from regular compliance services;

(c) large companies could make their own arrangements using GST approved IT protocols to access the GSTN system.

Small and Medium Tax Payers

Out of the expected 100 lakh registrants in the GST, more than 70 lakh are likely to file the returns directly to the common portal of the GST. The real challenge in the days ahead is to help the small and medium tax payers to file their returns. The GSTN has taken a number of steps to help them.

The invoice level data can be directly entered on the portal by the taxpayer. In case the number of B2B invoices is higher, he/she can use free offline tool developed by GSTN which imports data from Excel sheet and converts it into a 'json' file which is then uploaded on the GSTN portal. GSTN has already released a template of Excel sheet in which taxpayers can keep the business data at invoice level. The tool can pull up 19,000 line items from Excel sheet to generate a 5 Mb file. The tool can be used multiple times to upload data for creating GSTR-1. This obviates the need for continuous internet connectivity to file a return—a problem many small businesses may face in some of the small towns of India. With these facilities released by the GSTN, small and medium tax payers would need internet connectivity only at the time of the uploading of the return and not at the time of preparing of the return and its conversion into the standardised format from the Excel format. Further, it is also provided in the business rules that invoice details would be required to be uploaded only for B2B transactions and not for B2C transactions. Small tax payers can also take the help of Tax Return Preparers certified by the government much like the custom house agents who help the importer to suitably comply with the import formalities.

Large Tax Payers

For the larger tax payers with large volume of transactions, the GSTN has appointed GSPs who would assist in filing of returns as IT conduits. In order to work with GSPs, there is a requirement of Application Service Providers (ASPs) solution. Some GSPs have developed their own ASP solution to provide an end-to-end solution to assesses. ASPs will focus on taking taxpayers raw data on sales and purchases and converting it into GST returns (in case of multiple registrations, it is a huge task manually). These GST returns, or GSTRs, will then be filed on behalf of the assessee with GSTN via the GSP network. GSP provides a secured tunnel which feeds in data from ASP (in other words, ASP's output becomes input for GSP) to the GSTN and generates an acknowledgement. Companies dealing with large number of invoices every month need to automate and upgrade their ERP software to provide data points on a timely basis to cope with the increased number of returns. A good ASP-GSP is required to make the process of reconciliation under the GST regime seamless and hassle-free for large businesses.

Conclusion

Can we pull off this ambitious technology challenge? Two events in the past lend some confidence: Electronic voting machines were successfully installed and used in the elections in Uttar Pradesh and Bihar; and second, the Aadhar project has already delivered a unique biometric identification and number to 1,000 million Indians out of a total population of 1,250 million. These projects were executed against all odds.We are a raucous democracy, but we do have the ability to pull off this audacious technology challenge if there is national focus combined with political will. Both appear to be available in ample measure in the GST endeavour.

10

Impact of GST on Industry

GST is more than just a tax reform. It will change the business landscape creating pitfalls but also generating opportunities. It will trigger the formalisation of the informal economy and bring in documentary discipline. By ensuring in greater compliance, implementation of GST will provide comfort and succour to the honest taxpayer.

The business transformation will be triggered by three changes which are part of the GST design: abolition of the non-vatable central sales tax, abolition of the entry tax through deletion of entry 52 in the Constitution, and integration of the value chain, facilitating concurrent taxation by Centre and the States, across the value chain.

Trigger 1: The Abolition of CST

The CST was an origin based tax which was collected by the Centre and assigned to States where the goods were produced. The bulk of the revenues accrued to the large manufacturing state like Gujarat, Tamil Nadu and Maharashtra. As this tax could not be used to offset the VAT paid, cascading effect was not neutralised. The other interesting aspect was that in order to avoid the payment of the CST most of the manufacturing companies, especially FMCG companies', stock transferred their goods, creating state wise depots/warehouses. This is shown in Table 10.1.

The data for 2013-14 shows that stock transfers, on an average, accounted for as much of inter-state trade as the trade subject to the CST (in case of Gujarat and

Table 10.1
Impact of the Central Sales Tax

INR (in Crore)

Items	*Maha-rashtra*	*Tamil Nadu*	*Kerala*	*Karna-taka*	*Andhra Pradesh*	*Gujarat*	*Total*
Taxable turnover	316598	214771	293151	186045	60669	304479	1375713
Non-taxable turn-over (Stock transfer + consignment Sales)	241319	142321	44683	98300	160910	651620	1339154
Ratio of non-taxable to taxable turnover	76%	66%	15%	53%	265%	214%	97%

Source: Respective States Government's Revenue Division.

Andhra Pradesh, stocks transfers were more than twice as much). In other words, the distortion affected 50 per cent of the total trade that flowed between States.

The implementation of the GST will reduce these stock transfers and prod big companies to dismantle their warehouses built in each State and nudge them towards constructing lesser number of large warehouses either near procurement centres or close to market destinations. From the logistics point of view many of these companies could go in for larger multi axle trucks which can pick up goods from these large warehousing centres. The net impact could be lowering of logistics and warehousing cost. There would also be redistribution of manufacturing tax revenue from the bigger manufacturing states to the large consumption states of Uttar Pradesh and Bihar which can create some investment boom in these States. The manufacturing states would recoup some of their lost revenues from abolition of CGST through additional revenue from the services segment as these States are also service hubs. The company's manufacturing strategies will also need to factor in the second run of market expansion in these large poorer states of India.

Trigger 2: Abolition of Entry Tax will Create Significant Supply Chain Efficiencies and Lower Logistics Cost

There is ample evidence to suggest that logistic costs within India are high. One study suggests that, for example, in one day, trucks in India drive just one-third of the distance of trucks in the US (280 kms versus 800 kms). This raises direct costs (wages to drivers, passed on to the firms), indirect costs (firms keeping larger inventory), and location choices (locating closer to suppliers/customers instead of lowest cost location in terms of wages, rent, etc.). Further, only about 40 per cent of the total travel time is spent driving, check points and other official stoppages take up almost one-quarter of total travel time. Eliminating check point delays could keep trucks moving almost 6 hours more per day, equivalent to additional 164 kms per day—pulling India above the global average and to the level of Brazil. So, logistics costs (broadly defined, and including firms estimate of lost sales) are higher than the wage bill or the cost of power, and 3-4 times the international benchmarks.

Another study shows that inter-state trade costs exceed intra-state trade costs by a factor of 7-16, thus pointing to clear existence of border barriers to inter-state movement of goods. Further, inter-state trade costs in India exceed inter-state costs in the US by a factor of 6, suggesting that India's border effects are large by international comparison. Bringing India's inter-state costs down to the US level (reducing by a factor of 6) increases welfare by 15 per cent; conversely, completely eliminating intra-state trade frictions raises welfare by 5 per cent.

All of these barriers to inter-state trade become even more important in India because the share of roads in freight traffic is high (about 72%) and much higher than in comparable countries and rising over time because of under-investment in the railways.

Profitability in the manufacturing sector will be aided in a number of ways by the abolition of inter-state barriers:

a) lower logistic costs;
b) lower inventory cost facilitated by faster movement of goods through stimulation of the inter-state trade;

c) higher productivity growth through market expansion; and

d) lower of cost of procurement of intermediate inputs through better sourcing strategies unhindered by consideration of distance.

Trigger 3: The integration of the Value Chain for Taxation by Legally Empowering Centre to Tax Value Addition in Trading and States to Tax Manufacturing and Value Addition in Services

With a view to ensuring that tax credits are availed at every stages, large companies would prefer to buy from vendors who are part of the duty chain. Many industries may reduce the number of vendors they deal with and this will initiate a movement towards formalisation of the informal sector. The other possible consequence is the delayering in the trading segment of the value chain. The process of integration of the value chain would prod small traders to become part of the duty chain. Some of them may opt out, consumers could benefit from lower costs of distribution being passed on to them in the form of lower prices.

Overall on the manufacturing side, one would expect tax to turnover ratio for the large manufacturing companies to come down providing more resources for reinvestment.

Services Sector

The services segment of the business economy will face a higher tax incidence in view of the standard GST rate going up from 15 per cent (existing service tax rate) to 18 per cent. However, the net effective incidence of duty would be less than 3 per cent points, in view of the greater availability of input credit. Some large pan India services like banking, insurance and telecom could also face a greater compliance burden due to state wise registration. Hitherto, because service tax was only collected by the Centre, these sectors had opted for centralised registration with the central tax department. It would however be incorrect to look at the GST impact on services in isolation from its impact on manufacturing. There is considerable linkage between services growth and manufacturing growth.

Linkage between Manufacturing and Service Sector Growth

The Reserve Bank of India (RBI) in its report on *Currency & Finance 2001-02* had broadly divided the various services into three categories, which provides a useful analytical tool for analysing various services—their growth and revenue potential. These are: producer services, consumer services, and government services. The various individual services coming under each of these broad categories are given in Table 10.2.

Table 10.2

Category-wise Individual Services

S No.	*Category*	*List of Services*
1	Producer Services	Trade, Transport, Storage and Communication, Finance, Insurance, Real Estate and Business Services
2	Consumer Services	Hotels & Restaurants and other services like community, social and personal
3	Government Services	Public Administration and Defence

Table 10.2 shows that producer services are in the nature of intermediate services and have strong linkages to industry and this is also the area where significant service tax potential exists. The estimates made by the RBI in its report show that the elasticity of producer services with respect to industrial sector growth is 0.11 and the export of services also has a positive demand on producer services.

Because of the strong linkages between the manufacturing and the services sector, the services sector will benefit from the boost to manufacturing growth fuelled by GST. The extent of boost to the services sector will vary from sector to sector depending on elasticity of producer services with respect to industrial growth.

Macro Impact on Businesses

At a macro level, the big gain to businesses in India is the prospect of a stable tax regime. Individual states will no more have the power to raise tax rates except through the medium of the GST council. Any change in duty rates and exemptions would require consensus in the GST council. Getting three-fourth of majority in the GST council will not be easy. Businesses can now plan their investment secure in the belief that tax rates would remain broadly stable. This is also going to be a great incentive for foreign investment in India. All the triggers of growth which have been unleashed by the GST will make an attractive destination for foreign investment.

To utilise all the opportunities thrown up by GST, businesses would have to restructure their operations. They have to ensure that every rupee of tax credits in the supply chain is utilised by them. This would require each one of the businesses to carry out an impact assessment study. Closer integration of the business process engineering group with the tax team would benefit the company. Traditionally tax teams have been structured as separate verticals and such an arrangement would need to be replaced by centralisation of BPR (business process reengineering) and tax functions and promoting synergy between the two teams. Closer integration of the business process engineering group at the corporate headquarters with the tax team. Hitherto, tax team have been structured as separate verticals. Such an arrangement would need to be discontinued. Therefore centralisation of the BPR and the tax team may be beneficial.

There is also the other dimension of the strategic opportunities created by the GST design. This would be especially true in the area of structuring of contracts and the taking of advances. Companies would have to look at their invoicing procedure especially in the area of travel expenses of their employees. Centralisation of purchases and raising of invoices may also be necessary to utilise the credits. The phasing away of CVD (countervailing duty) would reduce the negative protectionism faced by the industry and this could make certain areas of business more profitable. Broadly the impact on industry is depicted as follows:

Impact on Industry

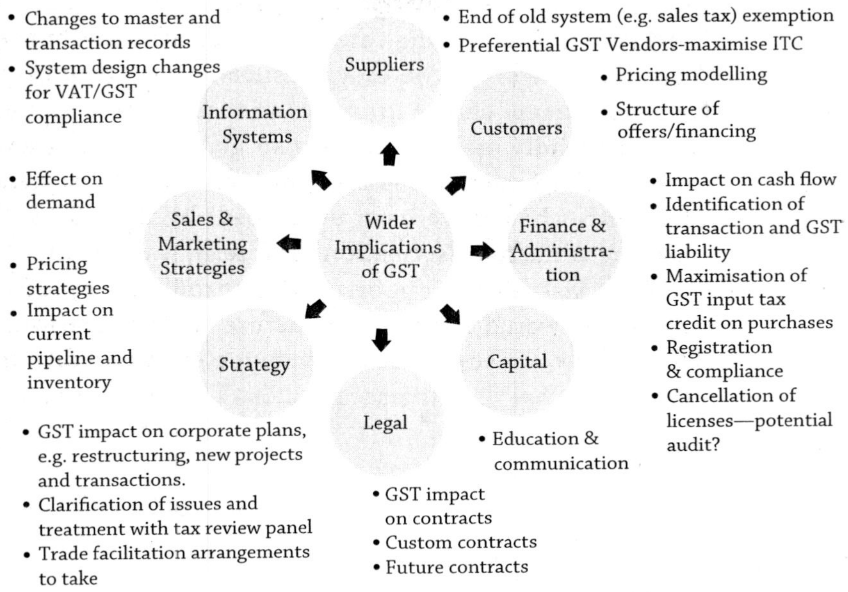

Business Preparedness

Seizing opportunities provided by GST would require internal preparedness. This is explained in the grid given below:

Getting Ready for GST

IT and Systems	*Organisation Restructuring*
• Inter linking of various systems	• Relationship between IT, finance & other business units
• Change in current system landscape & automation of tax recording	• Responsibility of management of GST systems
• Implementation of tax engine	• Management of GST processes/ manuals
• Information management	• Responsibility to ensure process/ documents are updated
• Updating billing system	
• Updating customer/ supplier/ tax code matters	• Centralised or de-centralised model of OST compliance and reporting
• E-invoicing & e-archiving	
• Extraction for compliance and reporting	

People & Change Management	*Accounting & Assurance*
• GST Responsibility in organisation	• Reconciliation between ERP systems and GST returns
• Resource gap (e.g. in terms of grades and skills) for GST-related roles?	• Automation of ERP systems for GST reporting
• Criteria for hiring GST-related roles	• Updation of master data and GL codes
• Recommended routes for hiring GST-related roles	• Review of process manuals and tax codes
• Staff training for handling GST-related roles	• Review of GST compliance
• How should performance measures (KRAs/ KPLs) at each grade within the GST function be defined	

Conclusion

GST is an opportunity and can translate into favourable business outcomes only when businesses can successfully marry business evaluation with businesses restructuring. Knowing where to go is extremely important. As the Roman Philosopher Seneca once said, "If you don't know to which port you are sailing, no wind is favourable".

III
Policy Prescriptions Going Forward

11

Expanding GST's Taxable Base

The structure of the GST approved by the GST council excludes the following sectors:

- alcohol;
- petroleum and energy;
- electricity;
- land and real estate;
- education; and
- healthcare

These exclusions do dilute from the flawless GST visualised by the Task Force constituted by The Thirteenth Finance Commission headed by Dr Kelkar. The Task Force had suggested the inclusion of all these items in the GST arguing that this would help in reducing the standard rates. The report prepared by Eva Van Leemput and Ellen A. Wieneck[1] for the Federal Reserve Bank recently showed that lower standard rates would amplify the welfare and growth effects of GST. The sector wise benefits of inclusion are explained below.

Petroleum

One of the significant achievement in the GST negotiation between the Centre and the States was that the Centre managed to persuade the States to include petroleum and petroleum products in the GST. However, five products namely, crude oil, petrol, diesel, aviation

---

1. Van Leemput, Eva and Ellen A. Wiencek (2017). "The Effect of the GST on Indian Growth", IFDP Notes. Washington: Board of Governors of the Federal Reserve System. 24 March. *https://doi.org/10.17016/2573-2129.29*

turbine fuel and natural gas were temporarily excluded from the GST net. The Centre and the States have been allowed in the interim to levy the pre-GST excise duties. To some extent, these transitional measures will help to ring fence Centres' and States' revenues from the revenue vagaries of GST implementation. Going forward however, there is great virtue in bringing all these within the ambit of the GST. Inclusion of diesel and petrol in GST would reduce the cascading effect in the logistic sector and enhance the gains from GST for user industries. Natural gas is an another petroleum products which is primarily an industrial intermediate for many industries and therefore its exclusion creates an overhang of cost for downstream user industries like chemicals, fertilisers and power generation. It also creates a dual system of GST and non-GST inputs preventing seamless flow of credit of taxes.

Electricity

Strictly speaking there is no bar on imposing GST on electricity. In the earlier central excise tariff, electricity was treated as goods and was nil rated in the tariff. The States today levy taxes on supply of electricity. There is a misconception that bringing electricity within the ambit of GST would lead to increase in electricity tariffs. On the contrary, imposing GST on electricity would help to offset duties, relating to capital goods and input goods and services. In the case of electricity supply, the embedded taxes are very significant (approx. 8%) largely due to taxes on raw materials (coal, renewables) and other equipment (solar panels and batteries). Not being part of the GST results in such embedded costs raising the final price of electricity. While these embedded taxes hurt manufacturers selling to the domestic market, they also hurt, in particular, exporters of electricity-intensive products, as such embedded taxes are not liable for any duty drawback. For exporters facing international competition, lower margins because of extra electricity costs could be damaging.

Mr Arvind Subramanian and Mr Navneeraj Sharma have made a very interesting argument to bring electricity into GST in their article titled "Bringing electricity in GST" published on 7 December 2017 in the *Indian Express*:

> Another argument calls for the inclusion of electricity in GST. Currently, there is a large bias in favour of renewables in GST policy. Inputs to renewables generation attract a GST rate of 5 per cent while inputs to thermal generation attract higher rates of 18 per cent. Supporting renewables might be conscious policy (and also good policy) but we are in a situation where subsidisation is proliferating across policy instruments, making it difficult to quantify the overall support. As we have discovered, complexity in GST rate structure arises because it is burdened with having to meet multiple objectives. Support for renewables should be direct, conscious, and transparent. GST should not become the instrument for adding (non-transparently) to that support.
>
> If electricity were to be included in GST, then there would be no discrimination between renewables and thermal energy because all inputs going into both forms of electricity generation would receive tax credits. GST would then become neutral between different forms of electricity generation as good tax policy should be.

Bringing electricity into the GST would entail revenue losses for both the States and the Centre as the blocked input tax credits accrues as revenue just like a withholding tax. The way out to compensate for these losses would be to impose a 5 per cent GST on electricity and allow pass through of blocked input tax credit through the GST pipeline but allow State governments to impose a small non-GST cess as a top up tax on the GST rate.

Bringing electricity into the GST therefore will be important to make Indian manufacturing more competitive. This is a small price to pay for some revenue loss.

Land and Real Estate

There has been a consistent reluctance on the part of the States to bring sale of land and buildings within the ambit of the GST. The conventional view was that bringing land under GST would require inclusion of immovable property in the definition of 'goods' in the constitution. A thorough analysis of the provisions of the GST law suggests that there is no constitutional bar to levy GST on supply of land and buildings

Stamp duty, which is levied under Article 268, is with reference to documents and is collected by the Centre on documents listed in Entry 91 of the Union List, and by the states on documents listed in Entry 63 of the State List. Therefore, the argument that the supply of the right of land and buildings cannot be subjected to GST because it attracts stamp duty is incorrect as stamp duty is levied on documents, while GST would be levied on the supply of land and buildings, whether as goods or services ("aspect theory" upheld by the Supreme Court in a host of judgements). Renting/leasing of land and buildings is subjected to service tax currently, but documents pertaining to such renting/leasing are subjected to stamp duty.

Entry 49 of the State List read thus:

"Taxes on Land and Buildings"

This entry might not be an impediment to levy GST on the supply of land and buildings because of the "aspect theory" as upheld by the Supreme Court; while the stock of land and buildings is subjected to tax by the states on the aspect of possessing land and buildings, the supply aspect can be subjected to GST (the taxable event is different in each case).

Levying GST would allow input credit duty on construction material used in the creation of immovable property. The question is how does one persuade the States. Currently, property tax is a source of revenue for urban local bodies. Land and building can be brought within GST without subsuming stamp duty which was major revenue worry for the States. This can be done by treating the supply of land and buildings as a supply of service rather than supply of goods. This line of reasoning is predicated on the premise that this supply of services can be provided either as works contract where the buyer gets land and real estate to build and develop the property or the services can be provided as sale of the already constructed property. Unfortunately in the pre-GST duty regime the law made an arbitrary distinction between work contracts and construction of residential and commercial buildings in which service tax is levied on the former and not on the later and no credit of input taxes was allowed on inputs such as iron and steel, cement and other fixtures which go into the construction of residential buildings. This can be resolved by treating supply of land and buildings as supply of services (sale of land or sale of the right to land could be treated as service). The inclusion of land and real estate in GST would require deletion of the entry from Schedule III of the CGST act which treats sale of land and buildings as neither supply of goods nor supply of services. An amendment would also be required in the provisions of the input tax credit rules which disallows input credit duty used in relation to land and buildings.

Bringing land and real estate in GST would be a very important step in cleaning up the land markets and could also strike a decisive blow against the black market menace. Some experts have opined that this alone would make what is currently a good GST into a great GST.

Healthcare

Bulk of the healthcare cost are in the nature of cost of medicines which are consumed by the poor section of society. Bringing health care within GST would help to offset taxes on medicines which carry an effective rate of duty of 9 per cent.

Rationalisation

The other important policy agenda would be to reduce the number of rates and duties. The present duty rate structure of 5 per cent, 12 per cent, 18 per cent, 28 per cent and 28 per cent plus cess introduces complexity in the system. As the Chief Economic Advisor puts it:

> One of the big virtues of a simple GST with one or at most two rates was that it would have abolished completely the distinction between goods and services (it would have been a lexicographer's dream and a GST bequest if a new word "goodsandservices" could have been created). Technology and the modern economy are blurring the distinction between the two. Our tax policy and system must reflect that. Tax authorities should not be burdened with distinguishing a good from a service. (A single rate will also avoid misclassification between goods and services.)

Given the rate structure that has been adopted, that is going to be difficult to achieve. But damage limitation will require that an overwhelming majority of the goods be taxed at the standard rate of 18 per cent, and nearly all services (with the exception of road transport) also be taxed at 18 per cent. If services are also allocated between the different rates, the result will be a messy system with multiple categories for both goods and services.

The rich poor argument advanced for having multiple rates do not carry much weight because many of the products consumed by the rich are produced by the poor. Further, the existing rate structure also has inbuilt an inverted duty structure especially in sectors like textiles, pharmaceuticals and tractor components. Therefore, there may be a case for combining the 18 per cent and 12 per cent rate slot into a single 16 per cent standard rate and do away with the 28 per cent slot. This would have the advantage of bringing a large number of consumer items which are presently in the 28 per cent duty slot to 16 per cent. This would stimulate demand for these items and give a fillip to manufacturing from the demand side. In order to balance the revenue position, the duty rate of gold could be raised from 3 to 5 per cent as already discussed in the earlier chapter. Gold and gold jewellery is largely consumed by the better off section of society. Lower GST rates on gold incentivises gold consumption and controverts government objectives of channelising and switching expenditure from gold to productive investment. The rationalisation of rates could be taken up once the GST revenues shows buoyancy and then the cess could be abolished and the sin goods could be slotted in the 40 per cent rate as suggested by the GST report. We would then have a simpler rate structure of 5 per cent, 16 per cent and 40 per cent.

Expansion of GST base and rationalisation of GST rates would make 'what is a good GST a great GST'. As the Chief Economic Advisor puts it: "The GST Council—a remarkable institutional innovation in the governance of cooperative federalism, and one that has proven to be so already in its first ten months of existence—will need to take up these challenges in the months ahead to take India from a good GST to an even better one".

12

GST and Exports

One of the interesting macroeconomic lesson is that no countries since the Second World War has grown consistently at more than 7 per cent without a 10 per cent plus growth in exports. India's attempts therefore to register high growth rates is therefore critically dependent on keeping our exports competitive. Table 12.1 illustrates the record of countries with high growth phases.

The global growth story shows that different countries witnessed high rates of growth at different periods but the common uniting factor was that high growth was propelled by high export growth. Japan in the 1960s, Thailand in the 1970s, South Korea in the 1980s, Malaysia and Vietnam in the 1990s and India more recently in the decade 2000-2010 exemplifies this.

Accurate data for China is difficult to get but some evidence available shows that China grew rapidly in

Table 12.1

Country-wise Growth Phases: 1960-1969 to 2000-2009

Countries	*1960-1969*	*1970-1979*	*1980-1989*	*1990- 1999*	*2000-2009*
India	-	-	-	-	8%+/20%+
Japan	10%+/16%+	-	-	-	-
South Korea	-	-	10%+/14%+	-	-
Thailand	-	7.5%+/10%+	-	-	-
Malaysia	-	-	-	7%+/13%+	-
Vietnam	-	-	-	7%+/20%+	-

Note: Average GDP growth rate/Average growth rate of exports of goods and services.

Source: Compiled by the author.

the 1990s and in the decade 2000-2010 on the back of robust growth in exports propelled by the stellar export performance of the foreign companies who invested heavily in the Special Economic Zone created by Deng Xiaoping in Southern China, using Hong Kong as the entrepôt. India therefore cannot rely on growing only through growth in domestic consumption and domestic investment alone.

There is another issue which also looms large. World Trade Organization allows exports subsidies for products only for economies whose per capita gross national income is below USD 1,000 (registered consistently for three consecutive years). India has recently crossed this threshold and therefore would be ineligible to grant export subsidies to products as they would run foul of WTO rules. In this situation, the only policy option is to ensure that all input taxes going into exports are refunded so that taxes are not exported. The evidence available shows that while Indian exports are zero rated, they are not zero taxed.

The GST presents a great opportunity to unlock these embedded taxes by providing for seamless flow of tax credit across the value chain. Unfortunately, while the GST does reduce the volume of embedded taxes, the present design of Indian GST does not completely eliminate this. This is because the GST rates and exemption regime still retains some exemptions and still excludes sectors like electricity, petroleum and real estate from the GST net.

Therefore, the Indian exports post GST still faces the problem of embedded taxes which would need to be refunded either through the drawback route or through schemes like ROSL (Rebate of State Levies) provided recently to the textile industry. These taxes gets embedded because of the following:

- Certain sectors like petroleum, electricity, land and real estate are kept out of GST.
- Duty Inversion—because input taxes are higher than taxes on value addition at the final stagewithin the GST.

- Certain duties embedded in inputs used in producing commercial crops do not get offset because the 'agriculturist' is defined in the GST law as not being a taxable person (for example in the case of cotton the taxes on inputs like seeds, pesticides, agricultural implements and tractors are embedded in the cost of cotton).
- Procedural changes under the GST like payment of IGST on imported machinery which used to be duty exempted in the old regime under the EPCG scheme.

These embedded taxes could vary between 1 and 7 per cent depending on the sectors and the value addition.

The strategy going forward to help Indian exports must therefore have the following three elements:

(1) The Central non-GST levies on petroleum must be factored in for calculating the duty drawback. In the case of the States, embedded taxes paid on petroleum, electricity and stamp duty should be refunded as part of the ROSL scheme with Centre sharing some of the burden.

(2) Within GST, accumulated credit happening on account of inverted duty structure and embedded taxes on inputs used in commercial agriculture crops like cotton and tobacco could be factored into drawback rate while State taxes flowing for the same reason could be included in the ROSL[1] scheme; and

(3) The GST exemption regime has done away with the duty free exemptions for capital goods under the EPCG[2] scheme. This has placed a heavy working capital burden on exporters. Here, the government could think of issuing an IGST exemption for such capital goods under the EPCG scheme. The government has temporarily agreed to this at its meeting on 6 October 2017 until a robust system for refund is put in place.

---

1. ROSL: Rebate of State Levies.
2. EPCG: Export Promotion Capital Goods.

These three measures would reduce the volume of embedded taxes and make our exports competitive to a great extent. The GST council will need to take a view on including the embedded GST taxes in both the drawback and ROSL scheme. At present, the ROSL scheme does not have a mandate to include refund of non-GST state levies and embedded taxes. The mandate has to be granted.

In the long run however, Government should speedily bring petrol, electricity, and land and real estate within the ambit of GST as has been argued in the previous chapter "Expanding GST's Taxable Base". This will not only make the GST a 'flawless GST' but will also reduce embedded tax on exports.

Conclusion

In the present global environment, when exports are slowly picking up, it would be a shame if we do not leverage the opportunity created by GST to boost exports through policy measures which are WTO compliant. We can grow more only if we export more.

13

GST and Reforms in Tax Administration

The GST success going forward will depend on effective reorganisation of the tax administration. Reforms in tax administration therefore have to go hand in hand with tax policy reforms.

GST implementation should spur both the Centre and the States to restructure their tax administration in consonance with the requirements of a modern tax administration. There are certain broad principles which can guide both the Central Board of Indirect Taxes and Customs (CBIC) and State Commercial Tax Departments in their reform effort.

First of all, all modern tax administration are built around ownership and functional responsibilities relating to key business processes rather than business entities.

The key business processes are:

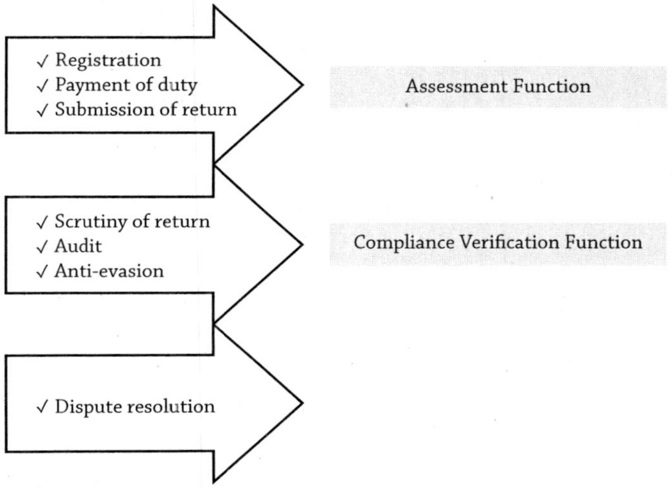

The first three processes constitute the assessment function while the next three are related to compliance verification function. In addition to this, modern tax administration must also create institutional arrangement for facilitation processes namely, training or capacity building and taxpayer services.

Each of these processes must have a functional owner and an administrative structure which can act as an interface between the field information's and the policy making body.

We can look at the existing setup of the CBIC and from their draw some lessons for revamping State Commercial Tax Departments.

Table 13.1

The Directorate Structure in the CBIC (Intermediate Layer Between the Board and the Field Formations)

Business Processes	*Function*	*Functional Owner*	*Remarks*
Registration Payment of Duty Submission of Returns	Assessment function	There is no functional owner for these three key business processes	Need to create a Directorate of Assessment
Scrutiny of Returns	Compliance verification function	No functional owner	Scrutiny of return could be made part of the function of Directorate of Assessment for it involves evaluating the correctness of assessment
Audit		Directorate of Audit	
Anti-Evasion		Directorate General of Anti-Evasion	
Dispute Resolution	-	Directorate of Legal Affairs	Partial ownership confined to dispute in Supreme Court and Delhi High Court
Facilitation Process	*Function*	*Functional owner*	*Remarks*
Training and Capacity Building	-	Directorate General of Training	-
Taxpayer Services		Directorate General of Taxpayer Services	Recently created

The CBIC needs to create a Directorate of Assessment which would also include the Return Scrutiny Process, for return scrutiny evaluates the correctness of assessment. This Directorate could have a role in suggesting change in the business rules pertaining to the assessment function. It could also oversee the preparation of Return Scrutiny Manuals. The Directorate of Legal Affairs could have a wider role of providing policy inputs to the Board on matters relating to dispute resolution. It could also have a role as a data depository for disputes in the Appellate and Tribunal forums.

State Commercial Tax Departments could create similar directorates which could own the various business and facilitation processes. These Directorates could act as an intermediate administrative layer for providing inputs to the Secretary (Commercial Taxes) for policy making.

The States Commercial Tax Departments also need to make a clear distinction between the three prongs of the compliance verification system, namely, return scrutiny, audit, and anti-evasion. In many of the commercial tax departments, the distinction between audit and return scrutiny is not clear.

The return scrutiny would largely cover the scrutiny of smaller units at the lower end of the turnover spectrum while the audit would focus on larger units and would require more specialised group of officers who have a mix of skills covering domain knowledge in taxation, accountancy and computer related skills. These distinctions have been explained in the earlier chapter on "GST and Compliance Verification".

One of the compliance verification concerns of both CBIC and State Commercial Tax Department is the need to have a strong compliance verification system to aid in revenue mobilisation without being administratively intrusive. This would require the creation of a strong risk assessment division which can select delinquent units for compliance verification based on risk parameters. This would ensure that honest and compliance units are not harassed. The risk assessment division could be separately created for return scrutiny under the Directorate of Assessment and for audit under the Directorate of Audit. The merit of the arrangement would be that the risk parameters in the case of return scrutiny would be extracted from the information furnished in the return while in the case of audit it could be derived from the audited annual financial returns submitted by the units at the end of the financial year. The risk parameters for the selection for audit would cover financial parameters like ratio of other income to total income or cash flow position which may have a bearing on non-compliance.

Anti-Evasion

The Directorate General of Anti-Evasion would require different kind of information for its role would be one of intelligence based investigations. The CBIC recently created a Directorate General of Analytics and Risk Management and attached it to Directorate General of Anti-Evasion. The Directorate would crunch the data from GSTN and also information received from Income tax departments. In November 2015, the CBIC and the CBDT had signed a formal Memorandum of Understanding to share specific information. Similar agreements could also be concluded with the States commercial tax departments.

Taxpayer Services

Like in the case of CBIC, States commercial tax department could also think of creating a 'Directorate of Taxpayer Services'. As the State governments largely deal with smaller units, a Small Taxpayer Unit could be created within the Directorate of Taxpayer Services to assist them.

Large Taxpayer Unit

The CBIC some years ago had created a LTU (large tax payer unit) in which direct tax and indirect tax officers were brought together to interact with larger units and provide better taxpayer services. The performance of the LTU has been mixed in the country. In the post-GST scenario, Finance Ministry could think of utilising the LTU structure to carry out joint audits of pan India services like banking, insurance and telecom services. The States in which the units are headquartered could carry out joint audits with the central GST officers. This would lead to single audits instead of multiple audits and ensure ease of doing business.

Dispute Resolution

Trade and industry have traditionally complained that their communication with the tax department has only been through the medium of a show cause notice. Disputes can be considerably reduced if there is uniformity in assessment practice. In this background, it may be a useful idea to create a 'Technical Secretariat' both in the CBIC and State commercial tax departments that would issue instructions on assessment matters which would be legally binding on the field officers. The GST law already has a provision to do this where the objective is to ensure uniformity of assessment practices across the country. The Central and the State government officials could meet periodically in biannual conferences in which both can exchange notes on assessment practices and forge a consensus on technical matters. This will be a great learning process for both and will bring Central and State tax officials together. The salutary consequence of this would be that dispute resolution would be much easier and the prospect of field officers talking different views across the country on similar matters would be greatly diminished. This would ensure that under GST we would not only have one nation, one market and one tax but also one common assessment practice on the same issue.

Business Reengineering Group

Finally, both the CBIC and the State Commercial Tax Department could also think of creating a central Business Reengineering Group which could periodically look at revisiting the ground rules for various business processes by incorporating best global practices. It could also play a key role in preparing standard operating manuals and revising them regularly for key business processes. The drafting of these manuals would be an important challenge going forward. The Centre and the States could take this up as a joint project. It is important that there is lucidity and clarity. Historically, a fine example was the drafting of the Indian Penal Code by Lord Macaulay in 1837. Even today legal pundits are fascinated by its relevance and its appreciation of local cultures and social behaviour. One of the interesting features of the Indian Penal Code was the use of live examples to illuminate the provisions of law. This is one lesson that can be carried into the drafting of GST manuals.

In conclusion, the importance of reforms in tax administration is sometime not fully appreciated and often treated as a poor cousin of tax policy. GST will yield fruitful results only if policy changes are underpinned by a modern tax administration. Only then will 'the rule of law' prevail over 'the rule of thumb' and 'principles will then become more important than 'principals'.

14

GST and Dispute Resolution

The GST law represents the collective consensus between the Centre and the States. While the law has many redeeming features, especially in the area of input credit, it has not gone far enough in the area of dispute resolution. One of the common grievances that taxpayers have in India relates to delays in the dispute resolution system. It is argued rightly that justice delayed is justice denied.

This argument has three aspects:

- When does a disagreement between the department and taxpayers take the form of a "dispute" in a legal sense.
- Once the dispute arises, how does one resolve it expeditiously with a degree of finality.
- When disputes involve principles of assessment (matters relating to principles of classification, valuation, etc.), how does one ensure that such decisions taken are uniformly applied all over the country

Flowing from the above, we can broadly outline the features of a world-class dispute resolution system:

- Disputes must be clearly defined and non-serious infringements should be kept out of the domain of disputes.
- Uniformity of practice in assessment must be ensured by facilitating those who draft the law to interpret it.

- The system must ensure speedy adjudication of cases within definite time lines.
- Taxpayers should be encouraged to settle disputes without resorting to litigation.
- Non-intrusive mechanisms of interactions must be created between the taxpayer and the tax department.

The implementation of GST law provides a great opportunity to create such a world-class dispute resolution system. Some of its provisions are truly a considerable improvement on the law as it stood earlier. For instance, the wide definition of 'input credit' would go a long way in relieving the assessee of the cascading effect of tax on tax. Similarly, the provision to give 100 per cent tax credit on taxes paid on capital goods is truly a radical change, going even beyond the practices of some countries in the European Union.

Fixing the dispute resolution system holds the key to easing the cost of doing business and will also help in attracting more foreign and domestic investment. One of the pain points today is the uncertainty in tax rates created by non-uniformity in assessment decisions taken by field officers.

To remedy the pain points a conceptual distinction must be made between 'offence cases' and 'assessment cases'. Offence cases are period specific and do not have recurring implications. Assessment cases, on the other hand, relate to principles of classification, valuation and eligibility of input tax credit and have recurring implications. Field officers could be allowed to decide offence cases on the basis of the facts available. On the other hand, a centralised system of binding instructions must be put in place for field officers for adjudicating assessment matters. In this connection, the CGST legislation in its chapter on Miscellaneous Provisions has a provision which must be made so as not to forbid any centralised competent authority from issuing binding instructions to any GST officer on genuine assessment matter.

It is, therefore, suggested that a technical secretariat may be created as a part of TRU (tax research unit) in the CBIC to issue such binding instructions on assessment matters to the field officers. Needless to say, the TRU is in the best position to interpret the law as it is associated with its drafting. It must also be provided that such cases relating to assessment matters must be adjudicated only by officers of the rank of Commissioner, without reference to monetary limits. The first appeal against the orders must go to the tribunal rather than the Commissioner Appeals, as this would help fast-track adjudications. In the Central Board of Indirect Taxes and Customs (CBIC), there is a feeling that such a proposal may create considerable disparity between the level of officers adjudicating similar cases in state governments as they tend to be bottom heavy in their administrative structures. To obviate this problem administratively, the Commissioner's powers of adjudicating assessment matters could be delegated to the additional commissioners.

The creation of a Technical Secretariat would help periodic discussion between the Centre and the states to look into contentious issues in assessment matters. Taxpayers will benefit from certainty in assessment matters, which would help in the ease of doing business and also reduce the cost of doing business.

The other important change is to do away with the distinction between suppression and non-suppression cases in the GST law and prescribe one uniform period of three years to complete adjudications. The suppression aspect could be addressed in the adjudication order on the basis of facts and a higher penalty could be imposed. Therefore, the penalty route may be a better way of dealing with this distinction rather than through a time period difference. This amendment will considerably reduce litigation as many taxpayers are incensed by wrong invocation of the suppression period and, therefore, opt to litigate rather than pay the tax.

Finally, to reduce the area of disputes a large number of minor procedural infringements could be subject to non-appealable administrative levies. In the GST law in the provisions relating to offences and penalties, the list of offences on which major penalties could be imposed is listed out so as to dilute the discretion of the field officers. This is a welcome provision. The chapter discusses the principles for imposing minor penalty. It is suggested that instead of imposing minor penalties, a list of cases of procedural infringements may be listed out and may be subjected to administrative levies. This would ensure that such cases are decided at the level of junior officers and do not clog the dispute resolution system.

These three changes in the GST law could help create a world-class dispute resolution system and make India an attractive investment destination.

15

GST and Institution Building

Economic research into the role of institutions in economic development was really triggered off by an important macroeconomic question which economists have long grappled with: why do some countries get rich and why do some remain poor?

Max Weber in his famous treatise attributed growth of western capitalism to the Protestant beliefs and ethics. China's recent growth diluted the strength of the Weber argument by showing that Confucian values could also promote growth. The Nobel Laureate Douglass North has been the pioneer in this area and his seminal work, "The Role of Institution in Economic Development" has provided useful insights into the question of why some countries grow faster than others. The crucial insight here is that what matters are the rules of the game in a society as defined by prevailing explicit and implicit behaviour norms and their ability to create appropriate incentives for desirable economic behaviour. Following this line of reasoning the success of Western capitalism is attributed to protection of propriety rights and the prevalence of the rule of law. "The Primacy of Institutions (and what this does and does not mean)" have taken this argument further. Their point is that while institutions are important in the development process, each function comes with its own array of choices. The appropriate choices to make could hinge on certain specific elements be it geography, political economy, initial conditions of growth or cultural norms. Here economic analysis may not be very helpful because trade-offs are involved which each society has to deliberate upon and decide. For example, we have the eternal question of how much regulation and how much of competition to allow?

The GST reform has been built on a unique institutional innovation namely the Empowered Committee of State Finance Ministers. The Committee was created in 2001 for implementation of State VAT and was registered under the Societies Act in 2004 as an institutional body. In a political master stroke, Yashwant Sinha made the Marxist Finance Minister from West Bengal Dr Ashim Das Gupta as the head of the Empowered Committee. He, thereby, started the tradition of appointing Finance Ministers from the Opposition ruled States to chair the Committee which has helped enormously in reaching a consensus and has strengthened the spirit of cooperative federalism. The Empowered Committee of State Finance Ministers delivered the State VAT in 2004 and has now delivered the design of the GST. The GST council is merely the morphed Empowered Committee of State Finance Ministers.

The GST council which is now the premier decision making body for indirect tax policy making is an example of pooled sovereignty. When all over the world we are seeing incessant demands for greater devolution of political and economic power (Scotland seeking to secede from Britain, Catalonia wanting to break away from Spain and Britain's recent decision to exit the European Union), in India we are witnessing a counter trend towards pooled sovereignty where the Centre and the States have voluntarily decided to give up their unilateral powers of levying indirect taxes and have agreed to jointly formulate indirect tax policy through the meeting of the GST council.

While these are welcome developments the implementation of GST, has created an institutional void at the level of the States. While the GST council at the national level will deal with the policy making, there is a need for a GST secretariat at the State level which would deal with the non-policy matters including implementation issues. Just as the Empowered Committee of State Finance Ministers was created in 2001, in 2017, the need was felt to create a GST secretariat in each State registered under the Societies Act with a permanent Secretariat and dedicated funding.

Senior indirect tax official from both the Central GST and the State GST (the existing commercial tax department) could engage in this institutional forum to discuss various issues including compliance verification and share risk assessment information. The States can benefit much from Centre's handholding especially in matters related to taxation of services which hitherto was handled by the Centre. Similarly, the Central officers can gain from the States experience in dealing with small traders and their non-compliant ways. This engagement will reduce the trust deficit between the Centre and State tax officials and forge the bonds of fiscal federalism. This can also be a useful forum for trade and industry to represent its problems jointly to Central and State officials on non-policy issues. In order to ensure its success, it is important that the GST council passes a resolution to establish such a State GST secretariat which should be followed up by the Cabinet Secretary writing to all the Chief Secretaries of States to start the process of creating them. In order to ensure the success of these Secretariats, both Centre and States need to provide funds on a joint sharing basis and dedicated staff for running a permanent secretariat as in the case of the Empowered Committee of State Finance Ministers.

Medium Term Institutional Innovation

International tax practices around the world do provide examples of replicable institution but as Dani Rodrik and Arvind Subramanian highlighted in their article "The Primacy of Institutions", the key to success is intelligent adaptation not blind replication. One institution worthy of imitation is the National Tax Payer Advocate which today functions in the United States. The institution of the National Tax Payer Advocate is a legal creature of the Internal Revenue Code and officers are drawn from the Revenue department. Every year the National Tax Payer Advocate is required to submit an annual report to the US Congress in which it identifies at least 20 issues/concerns of tax payers and after detailed study and research makes administrative and legislative recommendation to the US Congress. In 2012, the National Tax Payer Advocate had identified the following problems which provide a flavour about the concern of tax payers:

(1) The complexity of the Internal Revenue Code.
(2) The IRS is significantly underfunded to serve taxpayers and collect tax.
(3) The IRS has failed to provide effective and timely assistance to victims of identity theft.
(4) The IRS harms victims of return preparer misconduct by failing to resolve their accounts fully.
(5) Despite some improvements, the IRS continues to harm taxpayers by unreasonably delaying the processing of valid refund claims that happen to trigger systematic filters.
(6) The IRS's compliance strategy for the expanded adoption credit has resulted in excessive delays to taxpayers, has increased costs for the IRS, and does not bode well for future credit administration.
(7) The IRS's handling of ITIN applications imposes an onerous burden on ITIN applicants, discourages compliance, and negatively affects the IRS's ability to detect and deter fraud.
(8) The Preservation of Fundamental Taxpayer Rights is critical as the IRS develops a real-time Tax System.
(9) Overextended IRS resources and IRS errors in the automatic revocation and reinstatement process are burdening tax-exempt organisations.
(10) The IRS telephone and correspondence services have deteriorated over the last decade and must improve to meet taxpayer needs.

(11) The IRS has failed to make free return preparation and free electronic filing available to all individual taxpayers.

(12) The IRS is striving to meet taxpayers increasing demand for online services, yet more needs to be done.

(13) Challenges persist for international taxpayers as the IRS moves slowly to address their needs.

(14) The IRS lacks a service wide strategy that identifies effective and efficient means of delivering face to face taxpayer services.

(15) The IRS is substantially reducing both the amount and scope of its direct education and outreach to taxpayers and does not measure the effectiveness of its remaining outreach activities, thereby risking increased non-compliance.

(16) A proactive approach to developing a Government issued debit card to receive tax refunds will benefit unbanked taxpayers.

(17) The diminishing role of the Revenue Officer has been detrimental to the overall effectiveness of IRS collection operations.

This is an institution which we can replicate with some modification. The Government can create a National Tax Payer Advocate through an amendment of the Central Board of Revenue Act, 1958. The National Advocate General could be an IRS officer either from the CBDT or CBIC by rotation with one annual term. Like in the US, key issues of tax payer concern could be identified. The research work based on sample surveys could be done by the Tax Payer Research Unit (TPRU), a new body which has been created by the Ministry of Finance. Some research work can also be done through the NIPFP. The report prepared could be laid in parliament on the same lines as the *Economic Survey*.

Another useful idea is drawing up a Tax Payer Bill of Rights like in Canada. This could be made legally enforceable and will secure tax payer rights.

Taxpayer Bill of Rights

(1) You have the right to receive entitlements and to pay no more and no less than what is required by law.

(2) You have the right to service in both official languages.

(3) You have the right to privacy and confidentiality.

(4) You have the right to a formal review and a subsequent appeal.

(5) You have the right to be treated professionally, courteously and fairly.

(6) You have the right to complete, accurate and timely information.

(7) You have the right as an individual not to pay income tax amounts in dispute before you have had an impartial review.

(8) You have the right to have the law applied consistently.

(9) You have the right to lodge a service complaint and to be provided with an explanation of the findings.

(10) You have the right to have the cost of compliance taken into account when administering tax legislation,

(11) You have the right to expect us to be accountable.

(12) You have the right to have relief from penalties and interest under tax legislation because of extraordinary circumstances.

(13) You have the right to expect to publish a service standards and reports annually.

(14) You have the right to expect us to warn you about questionable tax schemes in a timely manner.

(15) You have the right to be represented by a person of your choice.

Commitment to Small Business

(1) The Canada Revenue Agency (CRA) is committed to administering the tax system in a way that

minimises the costs of compliance for small businesses.

(2) The CRA is committed to working with all governments to streamline service, minimise cost, and reduce compliance burden.

(3) The CRA is committed to providing service offerings that meet the need of small businesses.

(4) The CRA is committed to conducting outreach activities that help small businesses comply with the legislation we administer.

(5) The CRA is committed to explaining how we conduct our business with small businesses.

The Tax Payer Bill of Rights in the Indian context could be made a little more specific and could be enforced through tax tribunals which like Consumer Grievance Tribunals could be created by an Act of Parliament and given legal teeth.

Institution are important for sustaining reforms. The introduction of GST was facilitated by certain institutional innovations like the Empowered Committee of State Finance Minister. Going forward, the benefits of this transformational tax reform could be consolidated through creation of state level GST Secretariats. In the medium and long term, we need to move to the next step of addressing tax payer grievances through creation of the office of the National Tax Payer Advocate modelled on the US practice. Finally, drawing of up a Bill of Rights could secure rights of the tax payers.

To sum up, a vibrant democracy respects its voters, it must also dignify its compliant tax payers.

16

Conclusion

The implementation of the GST on 1 July is truly a trigger point for the Indian economy. As the impact of this tax reform unfolds, large areas of the Indian economy will be impacted. It will truly be a fertile ground for research by professionals ranging from economists to social scientists to students of the Indian political economy.

GST impact will be strongly felt by the economy. It will spur growth by:

- lowering the cost of investment, and
- by expanding the market.

Both these points require some elaboration.

Lowering the Cost of Investment

Under the pre-GST system, Union excise duty and State VAT was levied on all capital goods. But input tax credit was generally limited to manufacturing and no input tax credit was allowed for Union excise duty paid on capital equipment acquired for use in transportation, infrastructure, construction, and distribution sector because these sectors were outside the scope of excise duty which was applicable to manufacturing only. Similarly, no credit was allowed for State VAT levied on capital goods acquired by the services sector, for example, telecommunication, transport, finance, insurance and IT services.

GST provides a more seamless and efficient crediting of taxes paid on capital goods which could make capital goods cheaper by 12-14 per cent (because they are taxed at the standard rate of 12.5% currently by the Centre) and increase demand for capital goods, raising investment and thereby growth. Assuming an elasticity of investment demand with respect to price to be -0.5 per cent, GST, by allowing full input tax credit for capital goods, could raise investment in capital goods by 6 per cent, resulting in 2 per cent higher investment (as machinery and equipment account for around one-third of total investment), which in turn could lead to incremental growth of 0.5 per cent, assuming an incremental capital output ratio of 4:1.

GST is also likely to stimulate investment by lowering the Marginal Effective Tax Rate (METR). Internal studies done within the tax policy group at EY by Gaurav Ghosh shows that the METR is lowered by the very design of the GST which is a tax on consumption. GST improves investment incentives by eliminating taxes on intermediate and capital goods and transferring them to consumption. At the all India level, the GST reduces METR (from 27% to 21%). However, the beneficial impact of lowering of METR varies from sector to sector. Table 16.1 shows the sector wise impact of GST on METR rates.

Table 16.1

Impact of GST on METR: Sector-wise

	Overall	*Agriculture*	*Manufacturing*	*Electricity*	*Construction*	*Trade*	*Transportation*	*Finance*	*Other*
Current METR (%)	27.00	18.50	23.80	19.99	37.07	39.83	41.74	31.18	34.03
Estimated METR post GST (%)	21.33	18.33	17.62	29.25	26.93	27.78	14.12	16.48	25.95

Source: Internal study done and compiled by the Author.

As the table shows the benefit of lower METR is most significant in the transportation sector because of greater availability of tax credit on capital goods which was hitherto not available. Broadly, the services sector will benefit from the GST impact on METR. The reason for this is that manufacturing sector got the benefit of tax credits of central excise duty paid on plant and equipment installed in the factory. The services sector did not get this benefit which would now become available as explained in the earlier para. The sector which sticks out like a sore thumb is electricity. Here, one can make a strong case for inclusion of electricity in the GST. The present design of GST excludes electricity. This aspect was discussed in the earlier chapter on "Expanding GST's Taxable Base". Similarly, bringing real estate into the GST beyond the construction stage would further lower the METR on construction by making available tax credits on GST duties discharged on inputs like cement and steel and create an investment boom which could help in job creation.

Market Expansion

GST induced growth impulses will also come from the expansion of market in India. The abolition of Entry 52 in the Constitution effectively does away with the levy of entry tax by States. This tax was imposed by all the States on goods entering their territorial jurisdiction. This levy escalated the cost of goods as this tax was not off-settable against the output taxes. The entry tax had the impact of reducing the daily distance covered by trucks carrying goods in the country (280 km in India versus 800 km in US) and fiscal barriers also created a significant difference between inter-state and intra-state costs of trade. A study shows that this differential in India varies by a factor of between 7 to 16 and was far greater than differential in other countries such as US suggesting that India's border costs are far greater than world norms.

GST is thus expected to spur growth by expanding inter-state trade. Another study for the Federal Reserve System done in March 2017 by two economists Eva Van Leemput and Ellen A. Wiencek[1] reaches similar conclusions. The reasoning given by them was that demand is a function of prices. Trade barriers to the extent they lower prices help to expand the market by

1. Van Leemput, Eva and Ellen A. Wiencek (2017). "The Effect of the GST on Indian Growth", *IFDP Notes*. Washington: Board of Governors of the Federal Reserve System. 24 March. *https://doi.org/10.17016/2573-2129.29*

stimulating consumption. In addition, trade barriers prevent consumers from purchasing from the most productive producers leading to distortions in resource allocation. There could also be gains for producers through cheaper sourcing of intermediate products.

There is no doubt that growth gains would be much more if excluded items like electricity and real estate are brought within the ambit of the GST.

Non-compliance

GST would certainly help GDP growth and thereby also indirectly help in resource mobilisation for investment in important social sectors like education and health. The design of the GST will help to improve the tax to GDP ratio by improving compliance in the trading segment of the value chain.

Research evidence shows that non-compliance was high on the trading side in the pre-GST duty regime because traders failed to benefit from declaring their true turnover because the eligibility of tax credit was limited to the trading part of the value chain. In this segment, the exempted units tended to trade with other exempted units obviating the need for passing the tax credits. In the GST, the integration of the value chain from raw material to retail incentivises the traders to declare their turnover, for then he gets the benefit of credit of Central taxes paid on input goods, input services, capital goods and IGST paid on imports. The revenues gains will be more on the direct tax side because the traders GSTN registration numbers have the income tax PAN number embedded in this. It would be reasonable to expect that income tax returns of those declaring trading as their principal business would report higher turnover and hence pay more direct taxes. These revenues would come as personal income tax as this category in the income tax classification covers incomes reported by non-corporate entities. This will help the country move from its present level of tax to GDP ratio of 17 per cent to somewhere around 20 per cent which is the normal level in the other emerging market economies.

Equity Dimension

GST has an equity dimension as well. The poorer states of India like Uttar Pradesh and Bihar will see a significant increase in their tax revenues because the GST is a destination based tax in which the SGST revenues will accrue to the States where the final product is consumed. This is in contradistinction to the CST which is an origin based tax with tax revenues going to the State where the products are manufactured. Some manufacturing revenue lost by richer States of India will be made up by other sources of revenue because the richer states are also service tax hubs and therefore lot of the final consumption of services would take place in these states. Maharashtra is a good example of this where the loss of revenues due to abolition of octroi would be made up by more revenues accruing from GST paid on banking, insurance and other financial services. This would cover pan India services like banking and insurance, transportation and other producer services which are linked to manufacturing.

Transparency in the Actual Incidence of Taxation

One of the less appreciated outcomes of the GST implementation is the clear answer to the question—what is the incidence of taxation on a product? In the pre-GST era, this was not evident as the tax rate mentioned on the invoice did not reflect the actual tax burden borne by the consumer. This was because the final sales invoice carried only the prevalent state VAT rate on the items. The non-offsetted central duties embedded in the upstream basic price, was not reflected as a separate levy. For example, tractor in the pre-GST duty regime was exempted from central excise duty but because of the exemption, tractors carried an incidence of duty of 12 per cent which could not be set off because of the exemption at the final stage. The GST by phasing away the exemptions has minimised the volume of non offsetted taxes (embedded taxes) and also minimised the cascading effect of tax on tax. It is for this reason that the final invoice reflects the actual incidence of both the central taxes (CGST) and the state taxes (SGST) which is actually borne by the consumer.

The public perception about increase in prices post-GST is because many of the manufacturers did not lower the base price equivalent to the relief in embedded taxes and sought to maintain the same price level thereby reaping higher profits. This created the need for bringing in an anti-profiteering mechanism to deter such deviant tax behaviour.

The communication challenge here for the tax administration is to show that the final tax in the GST regime has to be compared with the aggregate of the State VAT rate reflected in the final invoice combined with the embedded central duty in the upstream cost. Only a comparison of the two can demonstrate the true change in the tax incidence post GST. The Chief Economic Advisor has put this point very clearly in his article in the Business Standard published on 4 April 2017. Another general point and one that will pose a communication challenge in this: tax rate is not the actual burden felt by the consumer. What you see is not what consumer gets. So, if the government imposes a GST rate that seems greater than today's rate (Excise plus VAT combined), it does not necessarily follow that the tax burden has gone up. The reason is that today (pre-GST) there are a lot of embedded taxes (the so called cascading). Under the GST, on the other hand, what you see will be close to what the consumers gets. So, if a product goes from being exempted today and attracts a GST rate of 5 per cent, it could well be (as in the case of many agricultural products) that there has been no increase in the consumer's actual tax burden.

Role of Tax Incentives

A very significant policy fallout from the implementation of GST is the whole area of tax incentives. There is now growing evidence that taxation is not an effective instrument to achieve socioeconomic objectives. Studies by the World Bank and IMF shows that tax incentives don't really work except in a few cases where incentives are effectively targeted as in the case of tax exemptions for research and development in specific sectors. In many cases, tax incentives are given where investments would have taken place even without these incentives as they are influenced by other non-tax factors like labour costs and size of the market. These studies have advocated some degree of expenditure switching from tax incentives to infrastructure development and measures to improve the legal and regulatory regime.

Even within taxation, indirect tax incentives would yield fewer benefits than direct taxes. This is because indirect tax in general falls on consumption and therefore does not affect investment behaviour. The multiplicity of tax rates in GST is justified on the ground of taxing the rich man's consumption at higher rates. The rich-poor argument is sometimes flawed because what the rich consume, the poor produce. Some indirect tax incentives/ disincentives could be justified in cases where only challenge is to stimulate demand for products produced in labour intensive industries like textile, leather and food processing or for reducing carbon emission in pollution creating sectors. Therefore, there may be a case for having fewer GST rates going forward (compressing the 12% and 18% into a single rate of 16% could be one option). In course of time, the 28 per cent rate could be abolished and we could move toward a 40 per cent rate for demerit goods without the compensation cess.

Political Economy

GST's biggest impact would be its influence on the political economy of the country. The world over global trends reflect rising feelings of sub-nationalism: demands for political and economic sovereignty by Quebec province in Canada, Scotland's demand for political exit from Great Britain, similar demands from the province of Catalonia in Spain and more recently Britain's proposed exit from the European Union. India presents a refreshing contrast where 29 States and 7 Union Territories have jointly abjured their rights to levy and modify indirect taxes and have opted for joint policy making with the Centre through the medium of the GST council. This is a great example of pooled sovereignty in a period of sub-nationalistic fervour and a clamour for de-globalisation. It is for these reasons that GST has been hailed as a transformational reform which will not only reform indirect taxes in India but also strengthen the federal polity and nurture the idea of cooperative federalism.

GST is therefore a reform which can be celebrated for many reasons. In fact one can do no better than paraphrase C.L.R. James's immortal lines from his famous book: *Beyond the Boundary*—"who knows GST who only GST knows".

IV
Annexures and Appendices

Annexure 1

GST Exempted Goods

Chapter/ Heading/ Sub-heading/ Tariff item	*Description of Goods*	*Rate*
	Live Animals, Animal Products	
0101	Live asses, mules and hinnies	Nil
0102	Live bovine animals	Nil
0103	Live swine	Nil
0104	Live sheep and goats	Nil
0105	Live poultry, that is to say, fowls of the species Gallus domesticus, ducks, geese, turkeys and guinea fowls.	Nil
0106	Other live animal such as Mammals, Birds, Insects	Nil
0201	Meat of bovine animals, fresh and chilled.	Nil
0203, 0204, 0205, 0206, 0207, 0208, 0209	All goods, fresh or chilled	Nil
0202, 0203, 0204, 0205, 0206, 0207, 0208, 0209, 0210	All goods [other than fresh or chilled] other than those put up in unit container and, (a) bearing a registered brand name; or (b) bearing a brand name on which an actionable claim or enforceable right in a court of law is available [other than those where any actionable claim or enforceable right in respect of such brand name has been foregone voluntarily], subject to the conditions as in the ANNEXURE I]	Nil
3	Fish seeds, prawn/shrimp seeds whether or not processed, cured or in frozen state [other than goods falling under Chapter 3 and attracting 2.5%]	Nil
0301	Live fish.	Nil
0302	Fish, fresh or chilled, excluding fish fillets and other fish meat of heading 0304	Nil
0304, 0306, 0307, 0308	All goods, fresh or chilled	Nil

0303, 0304, 0305, 0306, 0307, 0308	All goods [other than fresh or chilled] and other than those put up in unit container and, - (a) bearing a registered brand name; or (b) bearing a brand name on which an actionable claim or enforceable right in a court of law is available [other than those where any actionable claim or enforceable right in respect of such brand name has been foregone voluntarily], subject to the conditions as in the ANNEXURE I]	Nil
0401	Fresh milk and pasteurised milk, including separated milk, milk and cream, not concentrated nor containing added sugar or other sweetening matter, excluding Ultra High Temperature (UHT) milk	Nil
0403	Curd; Lassi; Butter milk	Nil
0406	Chena or paneer, other than those put up in unit container and,- (a) bearing a registered brand name; or (b) bearing a brand name on which an actionable claim or enforceable right in a court of law is available [other than those where any actionable claim or enforceable right in respect of such brand name has been foregone voluntarily, subject to the conditions as in the ANNEXURE I]	Nil
0407	Birds' eggs, in shell, fresh, preserved or cooked	Nil
0409	Natural honey, other than those put up in unit container and,- (a) bearing a registered brand name; or (b) bearing a brand name on which an actionable claim or enforceable right in a court of law is available [other than those where any actionable claim or enforceable right in respect of such brand name has been foregone voluntarily, subject to the conditions as in the ANNEXURE I]	Nil
0501	Human hair, unworked, whether or not washed or scoured; waste of human hair	Nil
0504	All goods, fresh or chilled	Nil
0504	All goods [other than fresh or chilled] other than those put up in unit container and, - (a) bearing a registered brand name; or (b) bearing a brand name on which an actionable claim	Nil
0506	All goods i.e. Bones and horn-cores, unworked, defatted, simply prepared (but not cut to shape), treated with acid or gelatinized; powder and waste of these products	Nil
0507 90	All goods i.e. Hoof meal; horn meal; hooves, claws, nails and beaks; antlers; etc.	Nil
0511	Semen including frozen semen	Nil

6	Live trees and other plants; bulbs, roots and the like; cut flowers and ornamental foliage	Nil
0701	Potatoes, fresh or chilled.	Nil
0702	Tomatoes, fresh or chilled.	Nil
0703	Onions, shallots, garlic, leeks and other alliaceous vegetables, fresh or chilled.	Nil
0704	Cabbages, cauliflowers, kohlrabi, kale and similar edible brassicas, fresh or chilled.	Nil
0705	Lettuce (*Lactuca sativa*) and chicory (*Cichorium spp.*), fresh or chilled.	Nil
0706	Carrots, turnips, salad beetroot, salsify, celeriac, radishes and similar edible roots, fresh or chilled.	Nil
0707	Cucumbers and gherkins, fresh or chilled.	Nil
0708	Leguminous vegetables, shelled or unshelled, fresh or chilled.	Nil
0709	Other vegetables, fresh or chilled.	Nil
0710	Vegetables (uncooked or cooked by steaming or boiling in water), frozen, other than those put up in unit container and, - (a) bearing a registered brand name; or (b) bearing a brand name on which an actionable claim or enforceable right in a court of law is available [other than those where any actionable claim or enforceable right in respect of such brand name has been foregone voluntarily], subject to the conditions as in the ANNEXURE I]	Nil
0712	Dried vegetables, whole, cut, sliced, broken or in powder, but not further prepared.	Nil
0713	Dried leguminous vegetables, shelled, whether or not skinned or split other than those put up in unit container and, - (a) bearing a registered brand name; or (b) bearing a brand name on which an actionable claim or enforceable right in a court of law is available [other than those where any actionable claim or enforceable right in respect of such brand name has been foregone voluntarily, subject to the conditions as in the ANNEXURE I]	Nil
0714	Manioc, arrowroot, salep, Jerusalem artichokes, sweet potatoes and similar roots and tubers with high starch or inulin content, fresh or chilled, dried, sago pith.	Nil

0714	Manioc, arrowroot, salep, Jerusalem artichokes, sweet potatoes and similar roots and tubers with high starch or inulin content, frozen, whether or not sliced or in the form of pellets other than those put up in unit container and, - (a) bearing a registered brand name; or (b) bearing a brand name on which an actionable claim or enforceable right in a court of law is available [other than those where any actionable claim or enforceable right in respect of such brand name has been foregone voluntarily], subject to the conditions as in the ANNEXURE I]	Nil
08	Dried makhana, whether or not shelled or peeled [other than those put up in unit container and, - (a) bearing a registered brand name; or (b) bearing a brand name on which an actionable claim or enforceable right in a court of law is available [other than those where any actionable claim or enforceable right in respect of such brand name has been foregone voluntarily], subject to the conditions as in the ANNEXURE I]	Nil
0801	Coconuts, fresh or dried, whether or not shelled or peeled	Nil
0801	Brazil nuts, fresh, whether or not shelled or peeled	Nil
0802	Other nuts, Other nuts, fresh such as Almonds, Hazelnuts or filberts (*Coryius spp.*), walnuts, Chestnuts (*Castanea spp.*), Pistachios, Macadamia nuts, Kola nuts (*Cola spp.*), Areca nuts, fresh, whether or not shelled or peeled	Nil
0803	Bananas, including plantains, fresh or dried	Nil
0804	Dates, figs, pineapples, avocados, guavas, mangoes and mangosteens, fresh.	Nil
0805	Citrus fruit, such as Oranges, Mandarins (including tangerines and satsumas); clementines, wilkings and similar citrus hybrids, Grapefruit, including pomelos, Lemons (*Citrus limon*, *Citrus limonum*) and limes (*Citrus aurantifolia, Citrus latifolia*), fresh.	Nil
0806	Grapes, fresh	Nil
0807	Melons (including watermelons) and papaws (papayas), fresh.	Nil
0808	Apples, pears and quinces, fresh.	Nil
0809	Apricots, cherries, peaches (including nectarines), plums and sloes, fresh.	Nil
0810	Other fruit such as strawberries, raspberries, blackberries, mulberries and loganberries, black, white or red currants and gooseberries, cranberries, bilberries and other fruits of the genus vaccinium, Kiwi fruit, Durians, Persimmons, Pomegranates, Tamarind, Sapota (chico), Custard-apple (ata), Bore, Lichi, fresh.	Nil

0814	Peel of citrus fruit or melons (including watermelons), fresh.	Nil
7, 9 or 10	All goods of seed quality	Nil
0901	Coffee beans, not roasted	Nil
0902	Unprocessed green leaves of tea	Nil
0909	Seeds of anise, badian, fennel, coriander, cumin or caraway; juniper berries [of seed quality]	Nil
0910 11 10	Fresh ginger, other than in processed form	Nil
0910 30 10	Fresh turmeric, other than in processed form	Nil
1001	Wheat and meslin other than those put up in unit container and, - (a) bearing a registered brand name; or (b) bearing a brand name on which an actionable claim or enforceable right in a court of law is available [other than those where any actionable claim or enforceable right in respect of such brand name has been foregone voluntarily, subject to the conditions as in the ANNEXURE I]	Nil
1002	Rye other than those put up in unit container and, - (a) bearing a registered brand name; or (b) bearing a brand name on which an actionable claim or enforceable right in a court of law is available [other than those where any actionable claim or enforceable right in respect of such brand name has been foregone voluntarily, subject to the conditions as in the ANNEXURE I]	Nil
1003	Barley other than those put up in unit container and, - (a) bearing a registered brand name; or (b) bearing a brand name on which an actionable claim or enforceable right in a court of law is available [other than those where any actionable claim or enforceable right in respect of such brand name has been foregone voluntarily, subject to the conditions as in the ANNEXURE I]	Nil
1004	Oats other than those put up in unit container and, - (a) bearing a registered brand name; or (b) bearing a brand name on which an actionable claim or enforceable right in a court of law is available [other than those where any actionable claim or enforceable right in respect of such brand name has been foregone voluntarily, subject to the conditions as in the ANNEXURE I]	Nil
1005	Maize (corn) other than those put up in unit container and, - (a) bearing a registered brand name; or (b) bearing a brand name on which an actionable claim or enforceable right in a court of law is available [other than those where any actionable claim or enforceable right in respect of such brand name has been foregone voluntarily, subject to the conditions as in the ANNEXURE I]	Nil

1006	Rice other than those put up in unit container and, - (a) bearing a registered brand name; or (b) bearing a brand name on which an actionable claim or enforceable right in a court of law is available [other than those where any actionable claim or enforceable right in respect of such brand name has been foregone voluntarily, subject to the conditions as in the ANNEXURE I]	Nil
1007	Grain sorghum other than those put up in unit container and, - (a) bearing a registered brand name; or (b) bearing a brand name on which an actionable claim or enforceable right in a court of law is available [other than those where any actionable claim or enforceable right in respect of such brand name has been foregone voluntarily, subject to the conditions as in the ANNEXURE I]	Nil
1008	Buckwheat, millet and canary seed; other cereals such as Jawar, Bajra, Ragi] other than those put up in unit container and, - (a) bearing a registered brand name; or (b) bearing a brand name on which an actionable claim or enforceable right in a court of law is available [other than those where any actionable claim or enforceable right in respect of such brand name has been foregone voluntarily, subject to the conditions as in the ANNEXURE I]	Nil
1101	Wheat or meslin flour other than those put up in unit container and, - (a) bearing a registered brand name; or (b) bearing a brand name on which an actionable claim or enforceable right in a court of law is available [other than those where any actionable claim or enforceable right in respect of such brand name has been foregone voluntarily, subject to the conditions as in the ANNEXURE I]	Nil
1102	Cereal flours other than of wheat or meslin, [maize (corn) flour, Rye flour, etc.] other than those put up in unit container and, - (a) bearing a registered brand name; or (b) bearing a brand name on which an actionable claim or enforceable right in a court of law is available [other than those where any actionable claim or enforceable right in respect of such brand name has been foregone voluntarily, subject to the conditions as in the ANNEXURE I]	Nil

1103	Cereal groats, meal and pellets other than those put up in unit container and, - (a) bearing a registered brand name; or (b) bearing a brand name on which an actionable claim or enforceable right in a court of law is available [other than those where any actionable claim or enforceable right in respect of such brand name has been foregone voluntarily, subject to the conditions as in the ANNEXURE I]	Nil
1104	Cereal grains hulled	Nil
1105	Flour, powder, flakes, granules or pellets of potatoes other than those put up in unit container and, - (a) bearing a registered brand name; or (b) bearing a brand name on which an actionable claim or enforceable right in a court of law is available [other than those where any actionable claim or enforceable right in respect of such brand name has been foregone voluntarily, subject to the conditions as in the ANNEXURE I]	Nil
1106	Flour, of the dried leguminous vegetables of heading 0713 (pulses) [other than guar meal 1106 10 10 and guar gum refined split 1106 10 90], of sago or of roots or tubers of heading 0714 or of the products of Chapter 8 i.e. of tamarind, of singoda, mango flour, etc. other than those put up in unit container and, - (a) bearing a registered brand name; or (b) bearing a brand name on which an actionable claim or enforceable right in a court of law is available [other than those where any actionable claim or enforceable right in respect of such brand name has been foregone voluntarily, subject to the conditions as in the ANNEXURE I]	Nil
1106 10 10	Guar meal	Nil
12	All goods of seed quality	Nil
1201	Soya beans, whether or not broken, of seed quality.	Nil
1202	Ground-nuts, not roasted or otherwise cooked, whether or not shelled or broken, of seed quality.	Nil
1204	Linseed, whether or not broken, of seed quality.	Nil
1205	Rape or colza seeds, whether or not broken, of seed quality.	Nil
1206	Sunflower seeds, whether or not broken, of seed quality.	Nil
1207	Other oil seeds and oleaginous fruits (i.e. Palm nuts and kernels, cotton seeds, Castor oil seeds, Sesamum seeds, Mustard seeds, Saffower (Carthamus tinctorius) seeds, Melon seeds, Poppy seeds, Ajams, Mango kernel, Niger seed, Kokam) whether or not broken, of seed quality.	Nil
1209	Seeds, fruit and spores, of a kind used for sowing.	Nil
1210	Hop cones, fresh.	Nil

1210 10 00	Hop cones, neither ground nor powdered nor in the form of pellets.	Nil
1211	Plants and parts of plants (including seeds and fruits), of a kind used primarily in perfumery, in pharmacy or for insecticidal, fungicidal or similar purpose, fresh or chilled.	Nil
1212	Locust beans, seaweeds and other algae, sugar beet and sugar cane, fresh or chilled.	Nil
1213	Cereal straw and husks, unprepared, whether or not chopped, ground, pressed or in the form of pellets	Nil
1214	Swedes, mangolds, fodder roots, hay, lucerne (alfalfa), clover, sainfoin, forage kale, lupines, vetches and similar forage products, whether or not in the form of pellets.	Nil
1301	Lac and Shellac	Nil
1404 90 40	Betel leaves	Nil
1404 90 60	Coconut shell, unworked	Nil

Prepared Food Stuffs, Beverages, Spirits and Vinegar, Tobacco and Manufactured Tobacco Substitutes

1701 or 1702	Jaggery of all types including Cane Jaggery (gur), Palmyra Jaggery; Khandsari Sugar	Nil
1904	Puffed rice, commonly known as Muri, flattened or beaten rice, commonly known as Chira, parched rice, commonly known as khoi, parched paddy or rice coated with sugar or gur, commonly known as Murki	Nil
1905	Pappad, by whatever name it is known, except when served for consumption	Nil
1905	Bread (branded or otherwise), except when served for consumption and pizza bread	Nil
2106	Prasadam supplied by religious places like temples, mosques, churches, gurudwaras, dargahs, etc.	Nil
2201	Water [other than aerated, mineral, purified, distilled, medicinal, ionic, battery, de-mineralized and water sold in sealed container]	Nil
2201	Non-alcoholic Toddy, *Neera* including date and palm *neera*	Nil
2202 90 90	Tender coconut water other than those put up in unit container and, - (a) bearing a registered brand name; or (b) bearing a brand name on which an actionable claim or enforceable right in a court of law is available [other than those where any actionable claim or enforceable right in respect of such brand name has been foregone voluntarily, subject to the conditions as in the ANNEXURE I]	Nil

2301, 2302, 2308, 2309	Aquatic feed including shrimp feed and prawn feed, poultry feed & cattle feed, including grass, hay & straw, supplement & husk of pulses, concentrates & additives, wheat bran & de-oiled cake	Nil
2306	Cotton seed oil cake	Nil

Mineral Products

2501	Salt (including table salt and denatured salt) and pure sodium chloride, whether or not in aqueous solutions or containing added anti-caking or free flowing agents; sea water	Nil
26	Uranium Ore Concentrate	Nil
2716 00 00	Electrical energy	Nil

Products of the Chemical or Allied Industries

2835	Dicalcium phosphate (DCP) of animal feed grade conforming to IS specification No.5470 : 2002	Nil
3002	Human Blood and its components	Nil
3006	All types of contraceptives	Nil
3101	All goods and organic manure other than those put up or enforceable right in a court of law is available [other than those where any actionable claim or enforceable right in respect of such brand name has been foregone voluntarily, subject to the conditions as in the ANNEXURE I] in unit container and, - (a) bearing a registered brand name; or (b) bearing a brand name on which an actionable claim	Nil
3304	*Kajal* [other than *kajal* pencil sticks], *Kumkum, Bindi, Sindur, Alta*	Nil
3825	Municipal waste, sewage sludge, clinical waste	Nil

Plastics and Articles Thereof, Rubber and Articles Thereof

3926	Plastic bangles	Nil
4014	Condoms and contraceptives	Nil

Wood and Articles of Wood; Wood Charcoal; Cork and Articles of Cork; Manufactures of Straw, of Esparto or of Other Plaiting Materials; Basketware and Wickerwork

4401	Firewood or fuel wood	Nil
4402	Wood charcoal (including shell or nut charcoal), whether or not agglomerated	Nil

Pulp of Wood or of Other Fibrous Cellulosic Material; Recovered (Waste and Scrap) Paper or Paperboard; Paper and Paperboard & Articles Thereof

4802 / 4907	Judicial, Non-judicial stamp papers, Court fee stamps when sold by the Government Treasuries or Vendors authorized by the Government	Nil
4817 / 4907	Postal items, like envelope, Post card etc., sold by Government	Nil
48 / 4907	Rupee notes when sold to the Reserve Bank of India	Nil
4907	Cheques, lose or in book form	Nil
4901	Printed books, including Braille books	Nil
4902	Newspapers, journals and periodicals, whether or not illustrated or containing advertising material	Nil
4903	Children's picture, drawing or colouring books	Nil
4905	Maps and hydrographic or similar charts of all kinds, including atlases, wall maps, topographical plans and globes, printed	Nil
4907	Duty Credit Scrips	Nil

Textile & Textile Articles

5001	Silkworm laying, cocoon	Nil
5002	Raw silk	Nil
5003	Silk waste	Nil
5101	Wool, not carded or combed	Nil
5102	Fine or coarse animal hair, not carded or combed	Nil
5103	Waste of wool or of fine or coarse animal hair	Nil
52	Gandhi *Topi*	Nil
52	*Khadi* yarn	Nil
50 to 55	*Khadi* fabric, sold through Khadi and Village Industries Commission(KVIC) and KVIC certified institutions/outlets	Nil
5303	Jute fibres, raw or processed but not spun	Nil
5305	Coconut, coir fibre	Nil
63	Indian National Flag	Nil

Articles of Stone, Plaster, Cement, Asbestos, Mica or Similar Materials; Ceramic Products; Glass And Glassware

6912 00 40	Earthen pot and clay lamps	Nil
69	Idols made of clay	Nil
7018	Glass bangles (except those made from precious metals)	Nil

Natural or Cultured Pearls, Precious or Semi-Precious Stones, Precious Metals Clad With Precious Metal and Articles Thereof; Imitation Jewellery; Coin

7113	Bangles of lac/ shellac	Nil

Base Metal & Articles of Base Metal

8201	Agricultural implements manually operated or animal driven i.e. Hand tools, such as spades, shovels, mattocks, picks, hoes, forks and rakes; axes, bill hooks and similar hewing tools; secateurs and pruners of any kind; scythes, sickles, hay knives, hedge shears, timber wedges and other tools of a kind used in agriculture, horticulture or forestry.	Nil

Machinery and Mechanical Appliances; Electrical Equipment and Parts Thereof; Sound Recorders and Reproducers, Television Image and Sound Recorders and Reproducers, and Parts and Accessories of Such Articles

8445	Charkha for hand spinning of yarns, including amber charkha	Nil
8446	Handloom [weaving machinery]	Nil

Vehicles, Aircraft, Vessels & Associated Transport Equipment

8802 60 00	Spacecraft (including satellites) and suborbital and spacecraft launch vehicles	Nil
8803	Parts of goods of heading 8801	Nil

Optical, Photographic, Cinematographic, Measuring, Checking, Precision, Medical or Surgical Instruments and Apparatus; Clocks and Watches; Musical Instruments; Parts and Accessories Thereof

9021	Hearing aids	Nil
92	Indigenous handmade musical instruments as listed in ANNEXURE II	Nil

Miscellaneous Manufactured Articles

9603	*Muddhas* made of *sarkanda*, Brooms or brushes, consisting of twigs or other vegetable materials, bound together, with or without handles	Nil
9609	Slate pencils and chalk sticks	Nil
9610 00 00	Slates	Nil

9803	Passenger baggage	Nil

Miscellaneous

Any chapter	*Puja samagri* namely,	Nil
	(i) *Rudraksha, rudraksha mala, tulsi kanthi mala, panchgavya* (mixture of cowdung, desi ghee, milk and curd);	
	(ii) Sacred thread (commonly known as *yagnopavit*);	
	(iii) Wooden khadau;	
	(iv) *Panchamrit*,	
	(v) *Vibhuti* sold by religious institutions,	
	(vi) Unbranded honey	
	(vii) Wick for diya	
	(viii) Roli	
	(ix) *Kalava (Raksha sutra)*	
	(x) *Chandan tika*	
-	Supply of lottery by any person other than State Government, Union Territory or Local authority subject to the condition that the supply of such lottery	Nil

Source: Compiled from CBIC website.

Annexure 2

GST Exempted Services

Agriculture Services

1. Agriculture services which are exempt under GST are as follows:
   (a) Cultivation of Plants
   (b) Rearing of all life-forms of animals, for food, fibre, fuel, raw material, or other similar products
   (c) Except the rearing of horses.
2. Or Agriculture produce by way of:
   (a) Agricultural operations directly related to production of any agricultural produce including cultivation, harvesting, threshing, plant protection or testing.
   (b) Supply of farm labour.
   (c) Process carried out at an agriculture farm including tending, pruning, cutting, harvesting, drying,

cleansing, trimming, sun drying, fumigating, curing, sorting, grading, cooling or bulk packaging and such like operations which do not alter essential characteristics of agricultural produce but make it only marketable for the primary market.

(d) Renting or Leasing of agro machinery or vacant land with or without a structure incidental to its use.

(e) Loading, Unloading, Packing, Storage or Warehousing of agriculture produce.

(f) Agricultural extension services i.e. research services.

(g) Services by any agricultural produce marketing committee or board of services provided by commission agent for sale or purchase of agricultural produce.

3. Services by way of Loading, unloading, packing, storage or warehousing of rice.
4. Services by way of Pre- conditioning, pre-cooling, Ripening, waxing, retail packing, labelling of fruits and vegetables which do not change or alter the essential characteristics of the said fruits or vegetables.
5. Carrying out an Intermediate Production process as job work in relation to cultivation of plants and rearing of all life forms of animals, except the rearing of horses, for food, fibre, fuel, raw material, or other similar products or agriculture produce.

Banking and Financial Sector

1. Services by way of:
   - Extending deposits, loans or advances in so far as the consideration is represented by way of interest or discount (other than interest in credit card services).
   - Inter se sale or purchase of foreign currency amongst banks or authorised dealers of foreign exchange or amongst banks and such dealers.
2. Services by an acquiring bank, to any person in relation to settlement of an amount up to two thousand rupees in a single transaction transacted through credit card, debit card or charge card or other payment card service.

Exemption Received by RBI from Outside India

1. Services received by RBI from outside India in relation to management of foreign exchange services.

Charitable and Religious Sector

1. Services by an entity registered under Section 12AA of the Income Tax Act, 1961 by way of charitable activities.
2. Religious activities by way of:
   (a) Conduct of Religious ceremony
   (b) Renting of precincts of religious place meant for general public, owned or managed by an entity registered as a charitable or religious trust either under sec 12AA of the Income Tax act, 1961 or a Trust or an institution registered under sec 10(23C) (v) or a body or authority covered under sec 10(23BBA) of the Income Tax Act subject to some exceptions.
   (c) Services provided by a specified organisation in respect of a religious pilgrimage facilitated by the Ministry of the External Affairs of the Government of India. (Kailash Mansarovar and Haj Pilgrimage)

Construction Sector

1. Services provided by way of pure labour contracts of Construction, Erection, Commissioning, installation, completion, fitting out, repair maintenance, renovation or alteration of:
   a. Civil Structure or
   b. Any other original works
2. Pertaining to the beneficiary-led individual house construction or enhancement under the Housing for All (Urban) Mission or Pradhan Mantri Awas Yojana.
3. Services of pure labour contracts of construction, erection, commissioning, installation of original work pertaining to a single residential unit otherwise than as a part of a residential complex.

Education and Training Sector

1. Services provided by an educational institute to its students, faculty and staff.

2. Services provided to an educational institute by way of:
   - o Transportation of students, faculty and staff
   - o Catering including any mid-day meals scheme sponsored by the Central Govt., State Govt., or Union Territory.
   - o Security or Cleaning or house-keeping services performed in such educational institution.
   - o Services relating to admission to, or conduct of examination by such institution; upto higher secondary.

Entertainment Sector

1. Services by an artist by way of performance in folk or classical art forms of Music, dance or theatre if the consideration charged for such performance is not more than Rs. 1,50,000 (Exemption not applicable to services provided by Brand Ambassador).
2. Services by way of right to admission to:
   - o Circus, dance or theatrical performance including drama or ballet,
   - o Award function, concert, pageant, musical performance or any sporting event other than recognised sporting event. Where the consideration for admission is not more than Rs. 250/- per person.
3. Services by way of training or coaching in recreational activities relating to:
   - o Arts or Culture, or
   - o Sports by Charitable entities registered under sec 12AA of the Income Tax Act.

Government Sector

1. Services by way of access to a road or bridge on payment of toll charges
2. Services by way of access to a road or a bridge on payment of annuity.
3. Services provided by Reserve Bank of India. (Services to RBI is taxable).
4. Services by a Foreign Diplomatic Mission located in India.

Services Provided by Government

1. Services provided by the Central Govt. or the State Govt. or Union territory or Local authority excluding the following services:
    a. Services provided by Department of Posts by way of speed post, express parcel post, life insurance, and agency services provided to a person other than CG, SG or Union territory.
    b. Services in relation to an aircraft or a vessel, inside or outside the precincts of a port or an airport.
    c. Transport of goods or passengers or
    d. Any service other than the services covered under entries above, provided to any business entity.
2. Services by a CG, SG, Union Territory, Local Authority or Governmental Authority by way of any activity in relation to any function entrusted to a Panchayat.
3. Services provided by CG, SG, Union Territory or Local Authority to a business entity with an aggregate turnover of upto twenty lakh rupees (ten lakh rupees in special category state) in preceding F.Y.
4. Services provided by CG, SG, Union Territory or a local authority where the consideration for such services does not exceed Five thousand Rupees.
5. Services provided by CG, SG, Union territory, or local authority by way of registration or certification as prescribed.
6. Services provided by CG, SG, Union territory, or local authority by way of issuance of passport, Visa, driving license, birth certificate or death certificate.
7. Services provided by CG, SG, Union territory, or local authority by way of allowing a business entity to operate as a telecom service provider or use radio frequency spectrum prior to April 2016.
8. Services provided by CG, SG, Union territory, or local authority by way of assignment of right to use natural resources to an individual farmer for prescribed activities.
9. Services provided by CG, SG, Union territory, or local authority by way of assignment of right to use any natural resources where such right to use any natural resource was assigned before 1st April 2016.

10. Services provided by Govt. entity to CG, SG, Union Territory, Local Authority or ay person specified by CG, SG, Union territory or Local Authority against consideration received from CG, SG, Union territory or Local Authority.
11. Services provided by CG, SG, Union territory, or Local Authority to another CG, SG, Union territory or Local Authority.
12. Services provided by CG, SG, Union territory by way of MOT charges on Import / Export.
13. Services provided by the CG, SG, Union territory or Local Authority by way of tolerating non-performance of a contract for which consideration in the form of fines or liquidated damages are payable.

Services Provided to Government

1. Services provided by Fair Price Shops to CG by way of sale of wheat, rice and coarse grains under the Public Distribution System (PDS) against consideration in the form of commission or margin.
2. Services provided by Fair Price Shops to SG or Union territory by way of sale of Kerosene, Sugar, Edible Oil, etc. under Public Distribution System against consideration in the form of commission or margin.
3. Services provided by the GSTN (Goods and Service Tax Network) to the Central Govt. or Union territory for implementation of GST.
4. Services provided to Govt. of article 243G in relation to any function entrusted to a Panchayat or article 243W to Municipality.
5. Services provided to the CG, SG, Union territory under any insurance scheme for which total premium is paid by the CG, SG or Union territory.
6. Services provided to the CG, SG, Union territory under any training programme for which total expenditure is borne by the CG, SG, Union territory administration.
7. Services provided to the CG by way of transport of passengers with or without accompanied belongings, by air, embarking from or terminating at a regional connectivity scheme airport, against consideration in the form of viability gap funding.

Other Government Sector

1. Services provided by Employees State Insurance Corporation to persons governed under the Employees State Insurance Act, 1948.
2. Services provided by the Employees Provident Fund Organisation to the persons governed under the Employees Provident Fund.
3. Services provided by IRDA to the insurers under the IRDA of India Act, 1999.
4. Services provided by SEBI set up under the SEBI Act, 1992 by way of protecting the interest of investors in securities to promote the development of and to regulate the securities market.
5. Services by way of collection of contribution under any pension scheme of the State Governments.
6. Services of leasing of assets by Indian Railways.
7. Services provided by the National Centre for Cold Chain Development under the Ministry of Agriculture, Cooperation and Farmers welfare.
8. Services by way of giving on hire to a state transport undertaking, a motor vehicle meant to carry more than twelve passengers or to a goods transport agency, a means of transportation of goods.
9. Services by State Government Industrial Development Corporations.
10. Transmission or distribution of electricity by an electricity transmission or distribution utility.
11. Services by way of contribution under the Atal Pension Yojana.
12. Services by way of assessment under the Skill Development Initiative Scheme.
13. Training services under Deen Dayal Upadhyaya Grameen Kaushalya Yojana.
14. Services provided by the incubatee up to a total turnover of fifty lakh rupees in a F.Y. subject to the below mentioned conditions:
    a. The total turnover has not exceeded 50 lakh rupees during the preceding F.Y. and
    b. A period of 3 years has not elapsed from the date of entering into an agreement as an incubatee.

Health Care Services

1. Health care services provided by clinical establishments or medical practitioner or paramedics are exempted under GST
2. Services provided by way of transportation of patients in an ambulance, other than covered in (a).
3. Services provided by cord blood banks by way of preservation of stem cellsor any other services in relation to such preservation.
4. Services provided by operators of the common bio-medical waste treatment facility to a clinical establishment by way of treatment of disposal of bio-medical waste or the processes incidental thereto.
5. Services provided by Veterinary clinic in relation to health care of animals or birds.

Legal Sector

1. Services provided by an arbitral tribunal to any person other than a business entity or a business entity with an aggregate turnover up to 20 lakh rupees (10 lakh in special category states) in the preceding F.Y.
2. Services provided by a partnership firm of advocates or Individual as an advocate other than senior advocate by way of legal services to:
   > An advocate or partnership firm of advocates providing legal services,
   > Any person other than a business entity or

> A business entity with an aggregate turnover of Rs 20 Lakh rupees (10 Lakh in special category states) in the preceding F.Y.

3. A senior advocate by way of legal services to any person other than business entity or business entity with an aggregate turnover up to 20 lakh (10 Lakhs rupees in the case of special category states) in the preceding F.Y.

Life/General Insurance Sector

1. Services of Life insurance business provided by way of annuity under the National Pension System regulated by the Pension Fund Regulatory and Development Authority of India under the Pension Fund Regulatory and Development Authority Act, 2013.

2. Services of Life insurance business provided or agreed to be provided by the Army, Naval and Air Force Group Insurance Funds to members of the Army, Navy and Air Force respectively under the Group Insurance Scheme of the Central Government.
3. Services of General Insurance Business under the prescribed schemes.
4. Services of Life Insurance Business under the prescribed schemes.

Renting of Immovable Property

1. Services by way of renting of residential dwelling for use as residence.
2. Services by way of a Hotel, inn, guest house, club or campsite by whatever name called for residential or lodging purposes, having declared tariff of a unit of accommodation below Rs. 1000/- per day or equivalent.

Services Provided by Sportsman to Recognised Sports Body

1. Services provided to a recognised sports body by:
   a. An individual as a player, referee, umpire, coach, or team manager for participation in a sporting event organized by a recognised sports body.
   b. Another recognised sports body.
2. Services provided by and to FIFA (Federation Internationale de Football Association) and its subsidiaries directly or indirectly related to any of the events under FIFA U-17 World Cup 17 hosted in India.
3. Services by way of right to admission to the events organised under FIFA U-17 World Cup 2017.
4. Services by way of sponsorship of certain sporting events organised by prescribed bodies.

Special Economic Zones

1. Exemption for goods or services or both imported by a unit or a developer in the Special Economic Zone from the whole of the integrated tax leviable thereon under sub section (7) of section 3 of the Customs tariff Act, 1975 for authorised operations.
2. (For the goods imported under SEZ, no IGST or Custom Duty will be levied on such).

Transport Sector

1. Services of transportation of passengers, with or without accompanied belongings by:
   (a) Railway in a class other than First Class or Air Conditioned coach.
   (b) Metro, Monorail or Tramway,
   (c) Inland Waterways
   (d) Public Transport other than predominantly for tourism purpose, in a vessel between places located India; and
   (e) Metered Cabs or Auto Rickshaws
2. Transport of Passengers with or without accompanied belongings by:

(a) Air Embarking from or terminating in an airport located in the state of Arunachal Pradesh, Assam, Manipur, Meghalaya, Mizoram, Nagaland, Sikkim, or Tripura or at Bagdogra located in West Bengal.

(b) Non-AC coach carriage other than radio taxi, for transportation of passengers, excluding tourism, conducted tour, charter or hire or

(c) Stage carriage other than air-conditioned stage carriage.

Transportation of Goods

1. Services related to transportation of goods by road are exempt from tax except the services of GTA (Goods Transport Agency) or Courier Agency.
2. Services related to transportation by way of inland waterways.
3. Services by way of transportation of goods by an aircraft from a place outside India up to a custom station of clearance in India.
4. Transportation in relation of following goods by Rail, Vessel & GTA are:
   (a) Agricultural Produce.
   (b) Milk, Salt and Food Grain, including floor, pulses, and rice.
   (c) Organic Manure.
   (d) Newspapers or Magazines registered with the registrar of Newspapers.
   (e) Relief Material meant for the victims of natural or man-made disasters, calamities, accidents or mishap.

(f) Defence or military equipment.

5. Transportation services by a Goods Transport Agency in relation to the following goods are exempt from the tax:
   (a) Goods where consideration charged for the transportation of goods on a consignment transported in a single carriage does not exceed one thousand five hundred rupees. or
   (b) Goods, where consideration charged for transportation of all such goods for a single consignee does not exceed rupees seven hundred and fifty.
6. Services provided by GTA to an unregistered Person including an unregistered casual taxable person, other than the following recipients, namely:
   (a) Any factory registered under or governed by the Factories Act, 1948.
   (b) Any society registered under the Societies Registration Act, 1860 or under any other law for the time being in force in any part of India.
   (c) Any co-operative society established by or under any law for the time being enforce
   (d) Anybody corporate established, by or under any law for the time being in force.
   (e) Any partnership firm whether registered or not under any law including association of persons.
   (f) Any casual taxable person registered under the Central Goods and Service Tax Act, or the Integrated Goods and Service Tax act or the State Goods and Service Tax Act or the Union Territory Goods and Service Tax Act.

Tour Operator

1. Services provided by a tour operator to a foreign tourist in relation to a tour conducted wholly outside India.

Exemption for the Services wherein Location of Service Provider is in a Non-Taxable Territory

1. Services received by a person from the service provider located in a Non-taxable territory by:
2. The CG, SG, Union territory, a Local Authority, a Governmental Authority, a commerce, industry or any other business or profession.

3. An entity registered under section 12AA of the Income Tax Act, 1961 (43 of 1961) for the purpose of providing charitable activities or
4. A person located in a Non-taxable territory but with below mention exceptions:
   a. Online information and database access or retrieval services by persons specified in above two entries.
   b. Services by way of transportation of goods by a vessel from a place outside India up to the custom station in India received by persons specified in the entry.

Miscellaneous

1. Services by way of transfer of Going Concern as a whole or an independent part thereof.
2. Services by an organiser to any person in respect of a business exhibition held outside India.
3. Services by an unincorporated body or Non Profit Entity registered under any law for the time being in force, or to its own members by way of reimbursement of charges or share of contribution:
   a. As a trade union
   b. For the provision of carrying out any activities which is exempt from the levy of Goods and Service Tax or
   c. Up to an amount of 5000 rupees p.m. per member for sourcing of Goods or Service from a third person for the common use of its members in a housing society or a residential complex.
4. Services provided by the IIM (Indian Institute of Management) as per the guidelines of CG to their studies by way of prescribed educational programs.
5. Intermediary services by the following persons in respective capacities:
   a. Business facilitator or Business Correspondent to a banking company with respect to accounts in its rural areas branch.
   b. Any person as an intermediary to a business facilitator or a business correspondent with respect to services mentioned in above entry. Or
   c. Business facilitator or business correspondent to an insurance company in a rural area.

6. Services provided by Biotechnology Industry Research Assistance Council.
7. Services by way of collecting or providing news by an independent journalist, press trust of India or United News of India.
8. Services of Public Libraries by way of lending of books, publications or any other knowledge enhancing content or material.
9. Slaughtering of Animals services.
10. Services by way of public conveniences such as provision of facilities of bathroom, washroom, lavatories, urinal or toilets.
11. Supply of services associated with cargo to Nepal and Bhutan (landlocked countries).
12. Exemption from Intra state supply of heavy water and nuclear fuels by the Department of Atomic Energy to the NPCIL from the entire central tax under sec 9 of the Central Goods and Service Tax Act, 2017.

Annexure 3

IGST Exemptions under GST

I. Multilateral/Bilateral Commitments—Imports by Privileges Persons, Organisations, Authorities and Foreigners

S. No	*Present Customs Notification No. and date*	*Gist of the Notification*
1	3/57-Customs, dated 08.01.1957	Goods imported by Diplomatic missions in India and their families, their personal and household effects, etc are exempted from import duties.
2	121/2003-Customs, dated 01.08.2003	All the equipments and consumable samples imported into India, by the Inspection Team of the Organization of Prohibition of Chemical Weapons, subject to the condition, inter alia, that such equipments shall be exported within six months of their import.
3	46/74-Customs, dated 25.05.1974	Exemption to Pedagogic materials imported by educational institutions, etc. in pursuance of the Customs Convention on the temporary importation of pedagogic material, subject to the condition that the goods are re-exported within 6 months from the date of importation.
4	84/71-Customs, dated 11.09.1971	Exemption to temporary import of Scientific equipments etc. by non-profit making scientific and educational institutions in pursuance of the Customs Convention on the temporary importation of scientific equipment, subject to the condition that the goods are re-exported within 6 months from the date of importation.

5	157/90-Customs, dated 28.03.1990	Exemption to specified goods imported for display or use at specified event such as meetings, exhibition, fairs or similar show or display, etc. which is being held in public interest and is sponsored or approved by the GoI or the ITPO [Schedule II events] or events organised by other organisations [Schedule III events] subject to the condition, inter alia, that the goods are imported under ATA Carnet for temporary admission and the said goods are re-exported within a period of 6 months from the date of importation.
6	148/94-Customs, dated 13.07.1994	Exemption to: (a) Foodstuffs, medicines, medical stores of perishable nature, clothing and blankets, imported by a charitable organization as free gift to it from abroad and meant for free distribution to the poor and the needy, (b) Goods imported by the Red Cross Society for purposes of relief to distressed persons, (c) Drugs, medicines and medical equipments required for the treatment of the victims of the Bhopal Gas Leak Disaster, (d) Goods imported by the Cooperative for Assistance and Relief Everywhere Incorporated (CARE) under the Agreement between the President of India and CARE. Supplies and equipments imported shall be re-exported when no longer required for the purposes and cannot be sold to a third party, (e) Goods imported into India for relief and rehabilitation purposes, in accordance with the terms of any agreement in force between the GoI and any foreign Government. These goods cannot be sold or otherwise disposed of in India except with the prior approval or subject to conditions as may be prescribed by the GoI. (f) Articles of food and edible material supplied as free gifts to the GoI by the agencies approved by the UNO or the EEC, (g) Articles donated to the GoI for use of defence personnel or donated to the National Defence Fund and dispatched by the Indian Mission in the country where they were donated, (h) Goods gifted or supplied free of cost under a bilateral agreement between the GoI and a Foreign Government.

7	154/94-Customs, dated 13.07.1994	Exemption to: (a) Samples in accordance with the International Convention to facilitate the importation of Commercial Samples and Advertising material drawn up at Geneva and dated the 7th day of November, 1952, (b) Price lists supplied free of charge in accordance with the Convention mentioned above, (c) Commercial samples upto ₹3 lakh in value in case of gem and jewellery industry and ₹1 lakh in case of any other industry, and not exceeding 50 units in number in a year, imported as personal baggage by bona fide commercial travellers or businessmen or imported by post or air, (d) Prototypes of engineering goods imported samples for executing or for use in connection with securing export orders subject to mutilation/re-export, (e) Bonafide commercial samples and prototypes value upto ₹10,000 and supplied free of charge.
8	104/94-Customs, dated 16.03.1994	Exemption to containers of durable nature subject to re-export within 6 months from the date of their importation.
9	9 22/2003-Customs, dated 04.02.2003	Exemption to: a) paper money; and b) wool, woollen fabrics and woollen apparels received as gifts by the Indian Red Cross.
10	151/94-Customs, dated 13.07.1994	Exemption to: (a) Fuel in the tanks of the aircrafts of an Indian Airline or of the Indian Air Force subject to the condition, inter alia, that the quantity of the said fuel is equal to the quantity of the same type of fuel which was taken out of India in the tanks of the aircrafts of the same Indian Airline or of the Indian Air Force, and on which the duty of Customs, or Central Excise had been paid; and the rate of duty of customs (including the additional duty leviable under the said section 3) or the rate of duty of Central Excise, as the case may be, leviable on such fuel is the same at the time of the arrivals and departures of such aircrafts; (b) Lubricating oil, imported in the engines of any aircraft registered in India or of any aircraft of the Indian Air Force; (c) Specified goods imported by the United Arab Airlines which will be carried on individual aircraft for use in hangars and which are flown back on the same aircraft; (d) Aircraft equipment, engines and spare parts imported by the Air India International or the Indian Airlines having been borrowed by the aforesaid airlines for fitment to their aircraft from foreign airlines outside India or from the foreign manufacturers of the prime equipment subject to the condition, that the said goods are being imported for fitment and re-export; and the said goods are re-exported within one month from the date of their importation into India.

11	130/2010-Customs, dated 23.12.2010	Exemption to printed ticket stocks, airway bills, any printed material which bears the insignia of the importing airline printed thereon including baggage tags, publicity material for distribution free of charge when imported into India by a designated airline.
12	10/2014-Customs, dated 12.05.2014	Exemption to specified goods, when imported into India for display or use at any specified event specified subject to the condition, inter alia, that the specified event is being held in public interest and is sponsored or approved by the Government of India or the India Trade Promotion Organization; and that the said goods are imported under an FICCI/TAITRA Carnet issued in accordance with the Agreement between the India-Taipei Association in Taipei and the Taipei Economic and Cultural Center in India on the FICCI/TAITRA Carnet for the Temporary Admission of Goods signed on 20th March, 2013 and the Carnet is guaranteed by the Federation of Indian Chamber of Commerce and Industry in India (hereinafter referred to as FICCI).
13	106/58-Customs, dated 29.03.1958	Exemption to goods imported by the Vice President of India on appointment or during his tenure of office. a) Articles for personal use; b) Food, drink, tobacco for consumption of Vice-President's household c) articles for furnishing d) motor cars for Vice-President's use
14	207/89-Customs, dated 17.07.1989	Exemption to foodstuffs and provisions (excluding fruit products, alcohol and tobacco) when imported into India by a person residing in India, not being a citizen of India subject to the condition, inter alia, that the CIF value of such goods imported in a year does not exceed ₹1 lakh.

15	39/96-Customs, dated 23.07.1996	Exemption to imports relating to defence and internal security forces. a) Medals and decorations imported directly by the GoI in the Ministry of Defence. b) Personal effects of the persons on duty out of India with the naval, military or air forces or with the Indian Navy or Central Para Military Forces if imported for delivery to the next of kin of such person if he dies or is wounded, is missing or is taken prisoner of war. c) Bona fide gifts from donors abroad when imported for the maintenance of war graves by an institution subject to certification by the Ministry of Defence. d) Imported stores purchased out of bonded stocks lying in a warehouse intended to be supplied free by the Government for the use of the crew of a ship of the Coast Guard Organization. e) Goods imported for trial, demonstration or training before any authority under the MoD or MHA in the GoI subject to certification by MoD or MHA and subject to the condition that the goods are re-exported within a period of 2 years from the date of importation. f) Goods imported by the National Technical Research Organization (NTRO). This exemption is valid till 31.12.2018.
16	153/94-Customs, dated 13.07.1994	Exemption to: 1. Articles of foreign origin for repairs and return, 2. Theatrical equipment including costumes for use by a foreign theatrical company or dancing troupe and re-exported thereafter, 3. Photographic, filming, sound-recording and radio equipments, raw films, video tapes and sound recording tapes imported in public interest and has been sponsored by the GoI and subject to certification by the Ministry of I&B and subsequent re-export, 4. Mountaineering equipments, materials, clothing, foodstuffs and provisions (excluding alcoholic drinks, cigarettes and tobacco), medical stores, imported by a mountaineering expedition and subject to re-export,
17	51/96-Customs, dated 23.07.1996	Exemption to research equipments imported by: (a) Public funded research institutions or a university or an Indian Institute of Technology or Indian Institute of Science, Bangalore or Regional Engineering College, other than a hospital, (b) Research institutions, other than a hospital, (c) Departments and laboratories of the Central Government and State Government, other than a hospital, (d) Regional Cancer Center (Cancer Institute), subject to, inter alia, registration with the DSIR.
18	8/2016-Customs, dated 05.02.2016	Exemption to goods imported for display or use at specified event [fair, exhibition] subject to re-export within 6 months from the date of clearance of the imported goods.

19	326/83-Customs, dated 23.12.1983	Exemption to: (a) Articles of gift received from any foreign government by Union or State Ministers and specified public servants and imported as baggage, (b) Articles of gift imported into India by a foreign dignitary, visiting India for any official purposes, as part of his baggage and to be gifted to Union or State Ministers and specified public servants.
20	146/94-Customs, dated 13.07.1994	Exemption to: (a) Challenge Cups and Trophies awarded to an Indian team in connection with its participation in a tournament outside India and brought by it into India for being kept with an Official Sports Association, (b) Medals and trophies awarded to members of Indian teams for their participation in international tournaments or competitions outside India, (c) Prizes won by any member of an Indian Team if the team has participated in any international tournament or competition in relation to any sport or game, with the approval of the GoI in the Department of Youth Affairs and Sports, (d) Trophy when imported into India by the National Sports Federation recognized by the Central Government or any Sports Body for being awarded to the winning team in the international tournament including bilateral tournament and World Cup event to be held in India.
21	43/96-Customs, dated 23.07.1996	Exemption to specified goods on which a manufacturing process was undertaken in India and which were exported out of India for carrying out further manufacturing process of coating, electroplating or polishing or a combination of one or more of these processes, as the case may be, when re-imported into India after completion of the said processes, from the customs duty leviable on the value of goods which were exported i.e. customs duty is leviable on the value of the fair cost of the said processes carried out abroad (whether such cost is actually incurred or not) and insurance and freight, both ways.
22	259/58-Customs, dated 11.10.1958	Exemption to Challenge cups and trophies: (a) Which have been won by any unit of the Defence Forces in India or by a particular member or members of such unit in a competition; or (b) Which are being re-imported and which before being exported has been won by any such unit or member or members of a unit in a competition; or (c) Which have been sent by donors resident abroad for presentation to or competition among such units or members of such units.

23	271/58-Customs, dated 25.10.1958 [Since superseded by Notification No. 17/2017-Cus dated 21-04-2017]	Exemption to articles re-imported by or along with a unit of the Army, the Navy or the Air force or a Central Para Military Force on the occasion of its return to India after a tour of service abroad subject to satisfaction of the Commissioner of Customs that these articles were exported by or along with such unit on the occasion of its departure from India on such tour.
24	174/66-Customs, dated 24.09.1966	Goods not produced or manufactured in India, which are private personal property and which prior to their import into India have been exported therefrom and re-imported within three years from the date of export.
25	158/95-Customs, dated 14.11.1995	Exemption to: (a) Goods manufactured in India and parts of such goods whether of Indian or foreign manufacture and re-imported into India for repairs or for reconditioning. (b) Goods manufactured in India and re-imported for reprocessing or refining or remaking. Subject to the condition, inter alia, that goods are re-imported within one/three years from the date of export [10 years in the case of Nepal and Bhutan]; that goods are re-exported within 6 months of re-import, etc.
26	241/82-Customs, dated 04.11.1982	Exemption to goods [on their re-import] not produced or manufactured in India and on which the duty of customs leviable has been paid at the time of their importation into India and which were exported out of India for the execution of a contract approved by the Reserve Bank of India in connection with any commercial and industrial (including constructional) activities. In the case of goods on which any alterations, renovations, additions or repairs have been executed subsequent to their export, IGST will be payable on the value equal to the cost of such alterations, renovations, additions or repairs while the goods were abroad.
27	94/96-Customs, dated 16.12.1996	Exemption to: a) re-import of goods exported under claim of any export scheme [drawback, rebate, bond, DEEC or EPCG, DEPB], b) re-import of goods sent abroad for repairs etc. c) re-import of cut and polished precious and semi-precious stones sent abroad for some treatment [para 4A.20.1 of the FTP] d) Import of parts components of aircrafts replaced or removed during the course of maintenance in a SEZ. For (a), for goods exported prior to 1st of July, the repayment will go to Centre in CVD account. For exports after 1st July, the IGST paid will be apportioned.

28	134/94-Customs, dated 22.06.1994	Exemption to specified goods, when imported into India for carrying out repairs, reconditioning, reengineering, testing, calibration or maintenance (including service), subject to the condition, inter alia, that a) the repairs, reconditioning, reengineering, testing, calibration or maintenance (including service) as the case may be, is undertaken in accordance with the provisions of section 65 of the Customs Act, 1962 (52 of 1962), and b) the goods repaired, reconditioned, reengineered, tested, calibrated or maintained (including service) as the case may be, are exported and are not cleared outside the Unit.
29	26/2011-Customs, dated 01.03.2011	Exemption to: (a) Works of art including statuary and pictures intended for public exhibition in a museum or art gallery; (b) Works of art namely memorials of a public character intended to be put up in a public place including, materials used or to be used in their construction, whether worked or not; (c) Antiques intended for public exhibition in a public museum or national institution;
30	273/58-Cusoms, dated 25.10.1958	Exemption to re-import of unclaimed postal articles which were originally posted in India and re-imported as unclaimed, refused or redirected.
31	117/61-Customs, dated 13.10.61	Exemption to engines and parts of aircraft, when re-imported into India after having been exported, from the customs duty leviable on the value of goods which were exported [customs duty is leviable on the cost of repair], which includes the charges paid for the materials as well as for labour, insurance and freight) in the following cases:- (a) Engines and certain specified parts which fail abroad and are re-imported. (b) Engines or certain specified parts sent abroad as a stand-by for replacement of a defective one and subsequently brought back to India in the same condition without being installed on an aircraft. (c) Engines and certain specified parts lent by an Indian company to a foreign Company.
32	26/62-Customs, dated 19.02.1962	Exemption to catering cabin equipments and food and drink on re-importation by the aircrafts of the Indian Airlines Corporation from foreign flights subject to the condition that the goods were not taken on board at any foreign port or place.
33	26/62-Customs, dated 19.02.1962	Exemption to catering cabin equipments and food and drink on re-importation by the aircrafts of the Indian Airlines

II. Exemption for Goods in Transit to and from Nepal Bhutan [Land Locked Countries] Notification No 38/96–Customs

S. No.	*Gist of the notification*
1	Goods imported; a) from foreign country for the purpose of exports to Bhutan or Nepal; b) from Bhutan or Nepal into India for exports to foreign Country.

III. Miscellaneous Exemptions—Notification No. 12/2012-Customs

S. No.	*Chapter/ Heading/ Subheading/tariff item*	*Description of goods*
414	85 or any other Chapter	Television equipment, cameras and other equipment for taking films, imported by a foreign film unit or television team
415	85 or any other Chapter	Photographic, filming, sound recording and radio equipment, raw films, video tapes and sound re- cording tapes of foreign origin, if imported into India after having been exported therefrom
418	85 or any other Chapter	Goods imported for being tested in specified test centres
448A	8802 (except 8802 60 00 that is space craft)	All goods [aircrafts, helicopters etc.]
449	88 or any other Chapter	The following goods, namely: (a) Satellites and payloads; (b) Scientific and technical instruments, apparatus, equipments (including computers and computer software), accessories, parts, components, spares, tools, mock ups and modules, raw materials and consumables required for launch vehicles and for satellites and payloads (c) Ground equipment brought for testing of
518	Any Chapter	Used bona fide personal and household effects belonging to a deceased person
519	Any Chapter	Goods imported through postal parcels, packets and letters, the CIF value of which is not more than one thousand rupees per consignment
520	Any Chapter	Archaeological specimens, photographs, plaster casts or antiquities, intended for exhibition for public benefit in a museum managed by the Archaeological Survey of India or by a State Government

IV. Exemption from IGST on Imports by a SEZ Unit or SEZ Developer for Authorised Operations

V. Exemption from IGST from Bonafide Passenger Baggage and Transfer of Residence

S. No	*Chapter/Heading*	*Item covered*
1	9803	Exemption from IGST 1. on goods imported by a passenger or a member of a crew in his baggage [Does not apply to motor vehicles, alcoholic beverages, tobacco and tobacco products] 2. on goods imported by a person of India origin on his return to India [Transfer of Residence Notification No 26/2016-Customs] 3. on one laptop imported by a passenger of 18 years or more age [Notification No. 11/2004-Customs]

Appendix 1

Business Rules for Registration

Registration is the first step in the establishment of a tax system. What registration does is that it identifies the tax payers including his premises and tracks him through a unique identification number. This information forms the core component of the registration document. The task in the GST was to do this through a two-fold processes:

(a) migrating the existing registrants of State VAT, Central excise and Service Tax—this works out to around 80 lakhs who migrated to the new system; and
(b) Registering new tax payer who have come into the tax net for the first time in view of the introduction of the GST; typical examples of this are the fabric manufacturers and purchasers of unmanufactured tobacco.

This registration data is useful for policy analysis for it provides an idea about the total taxable base. The first question to ask therefore is: who requires to be registered under the GST law? The pictorial representation below answers this question:

Person who requires to be registered under GST

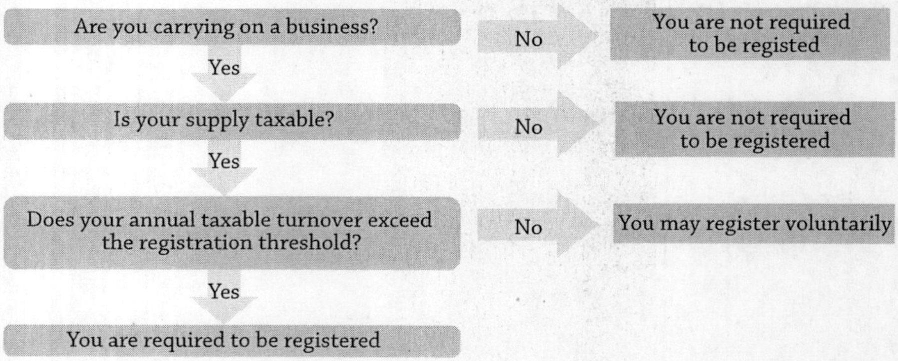

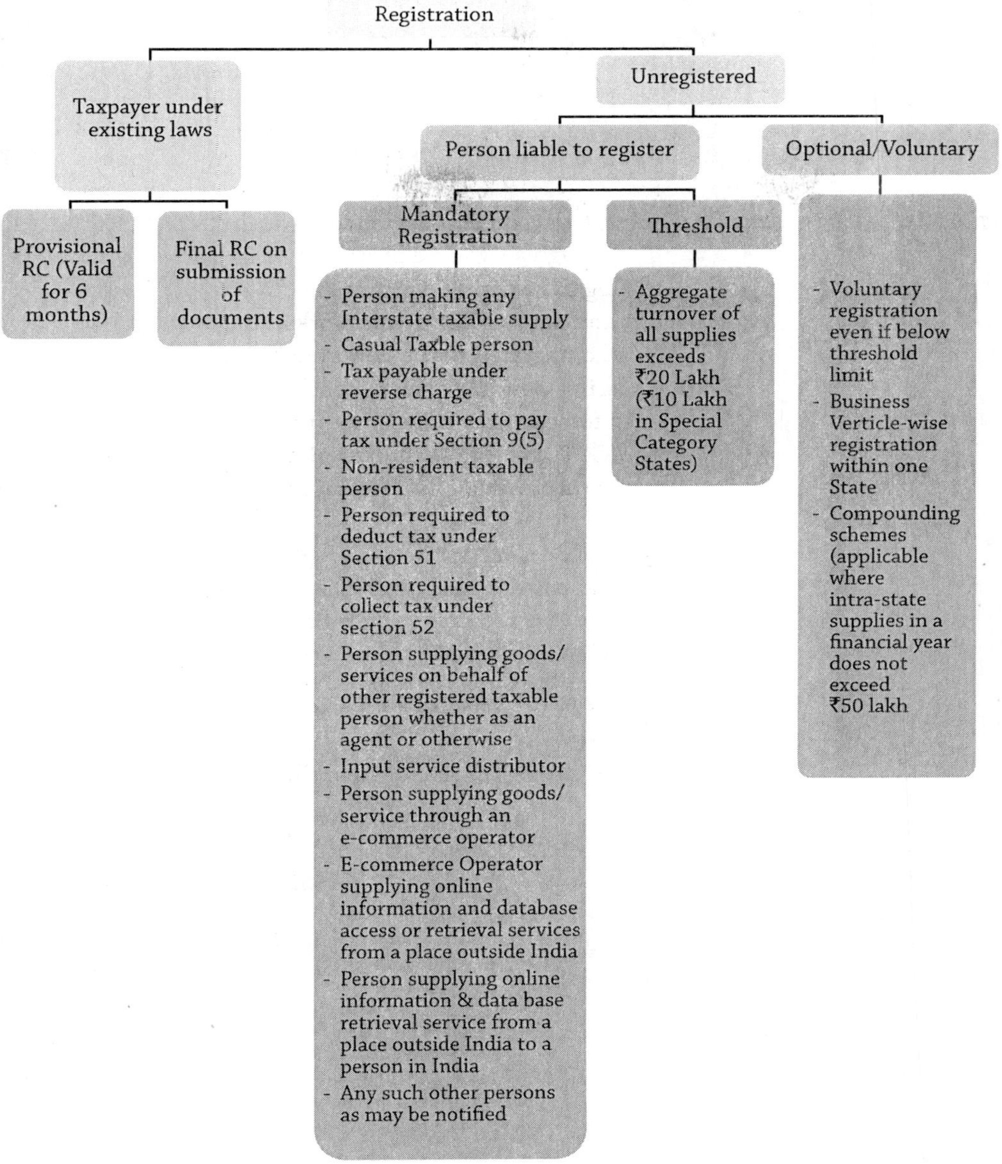

Persons exclusively making non GST or exempt supplies need not register.

There is also another category of registrants who are required to register irrespective of the turnover.

These are:

1. Persons making any inter-State taxable supply;
2. A casual taxable person, i.e., a person who occasionally supplies goods or services for furtherance of business and has no fixed place of business;
3. Persons who are required to pay tax under reverse charge;
4. Persons who are required to pay tax under sub-section 5 of section 9;
5. Non-resident taxable person;
6. Person who are required to deduct tax under Section 51, whether or not separately registered under this Act;
7. Persons who are required to collect tax under section 52, whether or not separately registered under the Act;
8. Person who supply goods and/or services on behalf of other taxable person whether as agent or otherwise;
9. Input service distributor, whether or not separately under the Act;
10. Persons who supply goods/or services, other than supplies specified under sub-section (5) of section 9 of IGST Act, through such electronic commerce operator who is required to collect tax at source under Section 56;
11. Every electronic commerce operator;
12. Every person supplying online information and database access or retrieval services from a place outside India to a person in India, other than a registered taxable person; and
13. Such other person or class of persons as may be notified by the Central Government or a State Government on the recommendation of the GST Council.

Procedure for Registration of New Applicant

Before applying for registration, every person other than the following:

a) Non-resident taxable person
b) A person supplying online information and data base access or retrieval services from a place outside India to a non-taxable online recipient of the IGST Act,
c) A person required to deduct tax at source and
d) A person required to collect tax at source,

shall declare in PART-A of FORM GST REG-01 on the common portal (*www.gst.gov.in*) either directly or through a notified Facilitation Centre the following details:

i. Permanent Account Number (PAN)
ii. Mobile number
iii. Email address
iv. State or Union territory (UT)

A Special Economic Zone unit or Special Economic Zone developer shall make a separate application for registration as a business vertical distinct from its other units located outside Special Economic Zone.

Every registrant is given a unique registration number which is PAN based. The first two digits identifies the State code. The next ten digits identifies the PAN number which is person rather than location centric. The thirteenth and fourteenth digit identifies the number of vertical segments registered by one legal entity (defined in terms of PAN number) within a State. The fifteenth digit is the check digit generated by the system using an algorithm which works on the first fourteen digits to generate the fifteenth digit. This ensures that errors while filing this number are avoided.

There are certain unique features of the registration process under GST which were earlier not contained in the Central and State registration procedures.

(a) provision for casual and temporary registration covering entities who may come from abroad to participate in a trade fair or an exhibition; this facility is also useful for those entities who do not have a fixed place of business; the central law currently does not have this provision while some States have;
(b) there is also a provision for de-registration of entity in case of persistent violation of provisions of the law; and
(c) The linkage between the registration number and the PAN number has been established in the GSTN registration code- this was absent in the case of State VAT registration which had a different unique identification number; this is an important provision for it links the indirect tax database to the direct tax database with salutary consequences for compliance verification.

To sum up, the registration procedures under the GST do away with manual modes. All registration is done online and the system allots a GSTN registration which is a pre-requisite for carrying out business transaction.

Appendix 2

Business Rules for Payment of Duty

The registration of a tax payer is a pre-requisite for payment of tax. It is for this reason that identification of tax payer and the delineation of the principal place of business becomes important. In the GST scheme the distinctive feature is that manual payment of taxes is done away with except for small payments of ₹10,000 and below per challan for a special category of tax payers including small and government departments. The payment of duty rules lay down a clear sequence of steps for payment. In this scheme the participating financial actors are the GSTN, the Reserve Bank, the tax payer and the State Treasuries.

In chapter 1 dealing with the design of the GST, a list of indirect taxes levied by both Centre and the States has been indicated which are subsumed in the GST. This plethora of tax has been replaced by three taxes namely—the Central GST, the State GST and the IGST for interstate supply. A taxable person is required to pay tax and also other payments in the form of interest penalty and fees.

To summarize, the following tax payments are required to be made:

(i) For any intra-state supply, taxes to be paid are:
   (a) CGST (Central Goods and Service Tax), that go to the account of the Central Government, and
   (b) SGST (State Goods and Service Tax) that go to the account of the State Government.

(ii) For any inter-state supply, tax to be paid is:
   IGST (Integrated Goods and Service Tax) which will have components of both CGST & SGST.

(iii) Payment of reverse charge on certain categories of supply of goods and services.

(iv) TCS (Tax Collected at Source) by Electronic Commerce Operator (ECO).

(v) Certain categories of registered persons are required to pay Tax Deducted at Source (TDS).

Who is Liable to Pay GST?

a) In general, the supplier of goods and/or services is liable to pay GST.

b) However, for certain categories of supplies, notified by Central or State Government, the liability to pay GST will be on the recipient under the reverse charge mechanism.

c) In certain cases, the liability to pay is on the third person, for instance, in the case of electronic commerce operator responsible for collecting tax at source and certain Government Departments responsible for deducting tax at source.

Utilisation of ITC for Payment of Output Taxes

i) input Tax Credit (ITC) is credited in the electronic credit ledger of the taxpayer (FORM GST PMT-2), on the common portal;

ii) The amount available in the electronic credit ledger can be used for making any payment towards output tax. No entry is allowed to be made directly in the electronic credit ledger. Any discrepancy in the electronic credit ledger will be communicated to the proper officer in FORM GST ITC-1 through the common portal;

iii) The amount of ITC available on account of IGST is first to be used to make payment towards IGST and the remaining amount can be used towards the payment of CGST & SGST, in that order;

iv) The amount of ITC available on account of CGST, is first to be used to make payment towards CGST and the remaining amount is to be used towards payment of IGST; ITC on account of CGST cannot be used towards payment of SGST;

v) The amount of ITC available on account of SGST, is first to be used to make payment towards SGST and the remaining amount will be used towards payment of IGST; ITC on account of SGST cannot be used towards payment of CGST; and

vi) For the payment of output tax which remains to be paid after the utilization of ITC credit and for payment of interest, fee or penalty or any other sum, payment is to be made through electronic cash ledger.

Mode of Payment

The GST provides for three modes of payment of tax:

(a) Payment through Internet banking and Credit/Debit card;

(b) Over the Counter payment (OTC) through authorized banks for deposits up to ten thousand rupees per challan per tax period, by cash, cheque, or demand draft (DD); and

(c) National Electronic Fund Transfer (NEFT) or Real Time Gross Settlement (RTGS) from any bank.

Mode-1: Payment through Internet banking and Credit/Debit card

(i) Every taxpayer who wants to avail the facility of e-payment will access GSTN common portal for generation of challan through which payment is to be made;

(ii) The registered taxpayer or a person authorized by him will login into the GSTN common portal (www.gst.gov.in). Some basic details of the taxpayer will be auto-populated such as:

a. Name;
b. Address;
c. GSTIN;
d. Email address;
e. Mobile number

(iii) The taxpayer will fill in the draft challan details of the taxes that are to be paid;

(iv) The challan so generated is a 14 digit Unique Common Portal Identification Number (CPIN), assigned only when the challan is generated. The challan once generated will be frozen and not allowed to be modified;

(v) A challan in FORM GST PMT-5 is generated by the common portal and is valid for a period of fifteen days;

(vi) Cash ledger and challan history is to be maintained in the GST Portal electronically;

(vii) Payment of CGST, IGST & SGST can be done through one single challan.

(viii) The challan has major heads for CGST, IGST, SGST and minor heads for Tax, Interest, Penalty, Fine, others;

(ix) No major-minor Inter head adjustment is allowed;

(x) GSTN will redirect the taxpayer to the website of the selected bank/payment gateway;

(xi) GSTN will redirect the taxpayer to the website of the selected bank/payment gateway;

(xii) GSTN will send an electronic string to the selected bank carrying the following specified details of the challan on real time basis:

a) GSTIN;
b) CPIN;

GST CHALLAN FORM						
Form No....... u/r ..... of the <State> Goods & Service Tax Rules, ...						
CPIN: 16020000000001	Date : 20/02/2016			Challan Expiry Date : 27/02/2016		
Mode of Payment (Payment through)						
☐ NeFT / RTGS			☑ Over the Counter			
Details of Taxpayer						
GSTIN: 07ASMCC9477Z1X3			E-mail Id: abc@xyz.com	Mobile No. : +91-9999999999		
Name: Kamath Traders Pvt. Ltd.			Address: 1234, Kamla Nagar, Delhi			
Break-up of Amount under different Tax Heads						
	Tax (0001)	Interest (0002)	Penalty (0003)	Fee (0004)	Others (0005)	Total
CGST (0001)	10000	10000	10000	10000	10000	50000
IGST (0002)	10000	10000	10000	10000	10000	50000
<Delhi> SGST (0003)						
Additional Tax (0004)						
Rupees (In words) : One Lakh Only					Total	100000

c) Challan amount;

d) Break-up of the amount into CGST, IGST & SGST heads;

e) State/UT Government to which SGST pertains.

(xiii) Taxpayer will need to make payment through internet banking, using the USER Id and Password provided by the respective bank;

(xiv) No change in the break-up or the total amount will be allowed at the bank's portal;

(xv) In case user wants to change the above fields he would have to abort the transaction and go back to GSTN portal to restart the process;

(xvi) On successful completion of the transaction, Electronic Focal Point Branch (e-FPB) of the bank will forward a Challan Identification Number (CIN) to GSTN on real time basis;

(xvii) The CIN is a unique 17-digit number containing 14-digit CPIN generated by GSTN for the particular challan and unique 3-digit bank reference number (BRN);

(xviii) The bank will also report the CIN to the taxpayer; the CIN is an indicator of successful completion of the transaction;

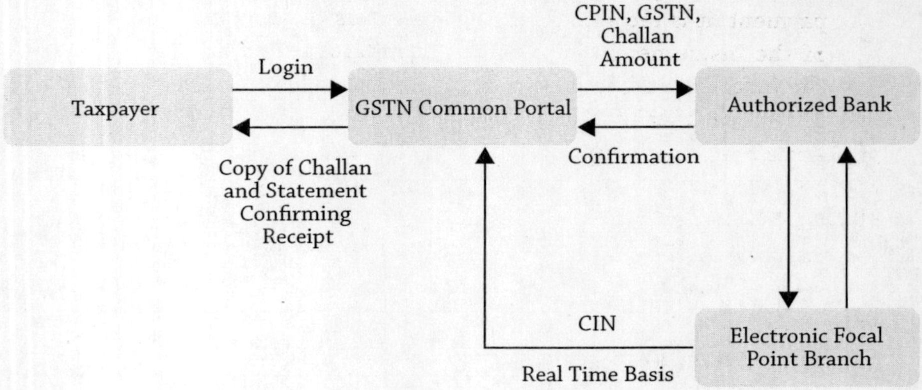

(xix) After successful e-payment there is an instantaneous reverse flow of information from the collecting bank to the GSTN common portal.

(xx) Upon receipt of confirmation from the bank regarding the completion of transaction, GSTN will inform the relevant tax authorities about the payment of taxes.

(xxi) GSTN will credit the taxpayer's electronic cash ledger in FORM GST PMT-4 which is maintained at the common portal; and

(xxii) The copy of paid challan with auto-populated CIN, date & time of payment and statement confirming receipt of amount by the bank is provided to the taxpayer by GSTN.

Mode-2: Over the Counter (OTC) Payment

OTC payment facility is only for deposits up to ₹10,000, per challan per tax period.

i. Every tax payer who wants to avail the facility of OTC will first have to login into the GSTN common portal (*www.gst.gov.in*);
ii. Upon creation of the draft challan, taxpayer will fill in the details of the taxes to be paid;
iii. Taxpayer will select the option of Demand Draft (DD)/Cheque/Cash based payment;
iv. Taxpayer has to provide details of the bank and its location (city/town/village) where the instrument/cash is to be presented (this is a mandatory field);

v. In case the taxpayer selects cheque/DD as the mode of payment, it is recommended that he enters the details of the instrument. This is not a mandatory field as the instrument may not be generated at the time of generation of challan;

vi. After the challan has been generated, it is frozen and non-modifiable; the CPIN is valid for fifteen days.

vii. GSTN will inform the challan details including its validity to the Core Banking System (CBS) of the selected bank on a real time basis;

viii. The challan is made available on the dashboard of the taxpayer in downloadable/printable form. If the taxpayer has selected DD/cheque as mode of payment, challan will have a disclaimer that 'payment is subject to realisation of cheque/DD';

ix. The taxpayer will bring forward the generated challan to the selected bank; the taxpayer should preferably carry with him two copies of the challan, one for bank records and the other for acknowledgement;

x. The taxpayer can also use a normal pay-in-slip and mention the CPIN & challan amount on the same for the payment of tax;

xi. If the payment is through cash or through instrument of the same bank, it will be realised immediately and CIN is generated immediately; the cashier will give the taxpayer a printed receipt from his system containing the CIN;

xii. If the payment is through instrument of some other bank with a branch in the same city the payment will

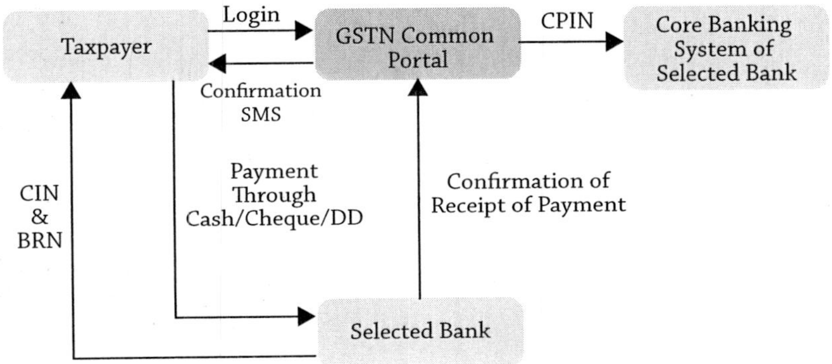

not be realised immediately; in such cases CIN is not generated immediately;

xiii. The authorised bank sends the instrument for collection and the transaction is treated as complete successfully only after the actual receipt of the said amount by the said bank;

xiv. The authorised bank will inform GSTN, through electronic string, and give the following details:
   a) CPIN;
   b) GSTIN;
   c) Challan amount;
   d) Banks acknowledgement number.

xv. On receipt of information from the bank, GSTN will send a message to the taxpayer;

xvi. Bank will send a second message to GSTN, once the cheque/draft is realised; on receipt of the second message, GSTN will send an SMS to the taxpayer, in addition to updating the status of the payment in the portal; and

xvii. If the cash ledger of the taxpayer is not updated within three days, the taxpayer should approach the bank where the instrument was deposited.

List of Banks Authorised by the Centre and the States

Allahabad Bank	Dena Bank	United Bank of India
Andhra Bank	Indian Bank	UCO Bank
Bank of India	Indian Overseas Bank	Vijaya Bank
Bank of Baroda	Oriental Bank of Commerce	State Bank of India
Bank of Maharashtra	Punjab National Bank	State Bank of Bikaner & Jaipur
Canara Bank	Punjab & Sind Bank	State Bank of Hyderabad
Central Bank of India	Syndicate Bank	State Bank of Mysore
Corporation Bank	Union Bank of India	State Bank of Patiala
IDBI Bank Ltd	State Bank of Travancore	

Mode-3: Payment through NEFT & RTGS from any Bank

Real Time Gross Settlement (RTGS) systems are specialist fund transfer systems where the transfer of money or securities takes place form one bank to another on a real-time basis. The minimum limit for fund transfer in case of RTGS is two lakh rupees.

National Electric Fund Transfer (NEFT) is also a fund transfer system where settlement takes place in batches and not individually. There is no minimum limit for fund transfer in case of NEFT.

Procedures:

(i) Every tax payer who wants to avail the facility of NEFT/ RTGS payment will first have to login into the GSTN common portal (*www.gst.gov.in*);

(ii) Upon creation of draft challan, tax payer will fill in the details of the taxes to be paid;

(iii) The taxpayer will chose NEFT/RTGS as the mode of payment;

(iv) Reserve Bank of India (RBI) itself will be the recipient of the amount transferred; therefore RBI will act as the authorised bank & e-FPB in this mode of payment;
In the view on the screen, against the name of the authorised bank, 'RBI' will be auto populated;

(v) The challan will have a unique CPIN & NEFT/RTGS mandate form attached with it. NEFT/RTGS mandate would have validity of fifteen days, same as that of the CPIN printed on it;

(vi) Upon successful saving of the challan details, the challan will be available on the dashboard of the taxpayer in downloadable/printable form. GSTN will also generate NEFT/RTGS mandate form in prescribed format and CPIN will be incorporated in "Account Name" field;

(vii) The payment in this mode would be permitted only by cheques and no cash payments would be permitted to initiate NEFT/RTGS transaction;

(viii) The NEFT/RTGS form will have the following details:
   a) IFSC code of RBI hosting the NEFT/RTGS account for GST;
   b) Account number of RBI's pooled account for GST;
   c) CPIN of relevant challan in "account name" field;
   d) Total tax amount;
   e) Sender to receiver remarks: GST Payment.

(ix) The form has a provision to write the NEFT/RTGS charges manually & then record the total amount to be collected by the bank i.e., the sum of challan amount & bank charges;

The entire NEFT/RTGS mandate form is auto-populated except the portion relating to charges.

(x) Thereafter, the taxpayer can print a copy of the NEFT/RTGS mandate form and approach his bank or any other bank for payment of taxes within a period of fifteen days;

(xi) GSTN will inform RBI on real-time basis about the following details:
  a) CPIN;
  b) GSTIN;
  c) Challan amount;
  d) Break-up of the amount into CGST, IGST, & SGST;
  e) State/UT Government to which SGST remittances pertains.

(xii) The accepting bank will add its charges for doing NEFT/RTGS remittance and collect gross amount from the customer;

(xiii) The amount indicated as GST amount for remittance will be transferred by the remitter bank to the designated account of the Government in RBI;

(xiv) For proper identification of the transaction a Unique Transaction Number (UTR) will be conveyed along with file details to RBI by the remitter bank;

(xv) Upon successful completion of the transfer at the end of the remitter bank, the remitter will get a receipt detailing the UTR;

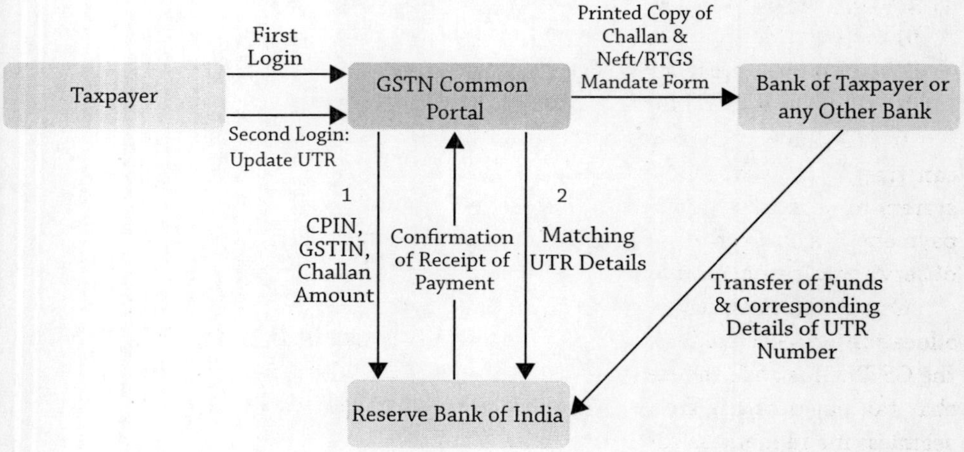

(xvi) The taxpayer will login back to GSTN portal and update the challan details along with UTR provided by the remitter bank for NEFT/RTGS transaction;

(xvii) On receipt of the transaction number, GSTN will communicate the UTR to RBI on real-time basis;

(xviii) Once RBI receives the payment, it will link the payment to the corresponding CPIN & UTR earlier received from GSTN and report the transaction to GSTN on real-time basis through an electronic string; and

(xix) Upon receipt of the electronic string on successful completion of the transaction by GSTN, the tax paid challan will be credited to the electronic cash ledger of the taxpayer in FORM GSTPMT-4.

GSTN will then lock the CIN so that it cannot be used again.

The entire mode of payment system adopted by the GST has the following advantage:

a) Electronically generated challan from GSTN Common portal for all modes of payment and nouse of manually prepared challan;
b) Facilitation for taxpayer by providing hassle free, anytime, anywhere mode of payment of tax;
c) Convenience of making online payment;
d) Logical tax collection data in electronic format;
e) Faster remittance of tax revenue to the Government account;
f) Paperless transactions;
g) Speedy accounting and reporting;
h) Electronic reconciliation of all receipts;
i) Simplified procedure for banks;
j) Warehousing of digital challan.

It will also confer an important benefit that Government can track duty payment on real time basis. In the present system while excise duty payment was monthly, the service tax payment was on quarterly basis. This created delay in reporting of service tax payment accurately.

One of the distinctive feature of the payment of duty is the allocation of IGST credit at the back end which is handled by the GSTN. This back end clearing mechanism has the advantage that tax payer at the front end can take input tax credit in seamless manner across the entire value chain.

A very significant improvement in the payment scheme is the handling of refunds. Tax payers have commonly conferred that excess payment made by them to the government whether State or Centre do not come back to them in time. Similarly refund of accumulated input credits for exports also takes time to be refunded. The GST therefore in that sense procedurally makes a significant breakaway from the current system. The rules provides that 90 per cent of export refund will be given upfront within 7 days and rest 10 per cent would be given within 60 days. This will considerably ease the working capital problem of exporters. The refund procedures also specify that products having inverted duty structure would be eligible for refund.

To summarize, the payment duty structure adopted in the GSTN system is in consonance with best internationally accepted principles and is based on strong IT platform which does away with manual methods and avoids physical interface between the tax payers and tax departments. In other words, "the tax will be collected like the bee collects honey from the flower with the minimum amount of disturbance. The sting is also taken away from the compliant that the bee stings."

Appendix 3

Business Rules for Scrutiny of Returns under GST

The tax return is an important document and is a medium for the tax payers to inform the tax department about the volume of his business transactions and his tax liability. In the GST scheme all the returns are filed electronically through the GST common portal enacted by the GSTN. The unique identification of each tax payer filing his tax return is ensured by the 15 digit GSTN registration number. At the time of granting of the GSTN registration number, the PAN number embedded in this GSTN number is verified with the Income tax database. More than 80 lakhs tax payers are registered. This number will grow as new registrants covering items brought into the tax net for the first time also get registered. The salient features of the Return submission procedure under GST are:

- filing of return would only be through online mode; though the facility of offline generation and preparation of return will also be available, the return prepared in the offline mode will have to be uploaded.

- there will be a common e-return for CGST, SGST, and IGST.
- a registered person can file GST Return through the common Portal (*www.gst.gov.in*) either himself or through his authorised representative.
- tax department will pull the return data relevant to it from the portal for further processing and analysis.

Who is Required to File Return?

The following categories of tax payers are required to file return under the GST regime:

a) Regular taxpayer (including casual taxpayer)
b) Composition Supplier/Compounding taxpayer
c) Non-resident taxable person
d) Input Service Distributor (ISD)
e) TDS deductor
f) E-commerce operator (ECO)
g) Government Departments and United Nation (UN) bodies

New System of Returns Filing

The GST council in its 27th meeting approved the principles for filing of new return design based on the recommendations of the Group of Ministers on IT simplification.

The key elements of the new return design are as follows:

Monthly Return

All taxpayers excluding a few exceptions like composition dealer shall file one monthly return. Return filing dates shall be staggered based on the turnover of the registered person. It is proposed that invoices for supply in a month be uploaded by 10th of the next month and large taxpayers may be directed to file return by 20th of the next month whereas the smaller taxpayers shall be given option to file return by 25th of the next month. Taxpayers who have no output tax liability and no input tax credit in any quarter of the financial year shall be given facility to file one NIL return for the entire quarter.

Unidirectional Flow of Document

For availing credit an invoice uploaded by the seller shall be the valid document. There shall be no to and fro movement of invoice data and stepwise collation of data like in GSTR-1→ GSTR-2A→ GSTR-2→ GSTR-1A→ GSTR-3 process.

Continuous Upload and Viewing of Invoices

Supplier shall be allowed to upload the invoices continuously anytime during the month and the recipient of the supply would also be able to continuously see the uploaded invoice.

Transition

There will be a three stage transition period in the process of the new return design getting fully implemented.

In stage one, the present system of filing of return GSTR 3B and GSTR 1 shall continue. As GSTR 2 and GSTR 3 are suspended, appropriate mechanism to close the assessment cycle would be worked out for this stage.

In stage two, GSTR 3B would continue and new return design would also come into operation. Provisional credit would continue to be available during this stage through GSTR 3B. GSTR 1 would stand withdrawn in the second stage. Information in relation to credit on missing invoice and rejected invoice may be collected during this stage and an option created in law to impose a fees on availing provisional input tax credit on missing invoices. This option would be exercised, if the provisional credit does not come down over a period of time which is necessary for completing the transition.

In stage three, GSTR 3B would be withdrawn and also the facility for provisional credit would get withdrawn. The only return in operation thereafter would be the new return thus completing the transition. It is expected that stage two would not last for a period longer than six months. The details of the transition on above lines would be worked out in consultation with IT team and law committee.

No Provisional Credit After the Transition Period

It may be noted that there shall be no concept of provisional credit after the transition period is over and new return design gets fully operational. Input tax credit would be available only on the seller uploaded invoices.

No System Based Credit Matching

There shall be no system based matching of input tax credit meaning that there shall be any need to upload both sales and purchase invoice by every dealer which is matched at the backend by the IT system. Acceptance of B2B invoice by the buyer on being uploaded by the seller shall form key

feature ensuring that credit flow is based on invoices which represent agreed supply between the buyer and supplier. To simplify acceptance of invoices by the buyer, concept of deemed acceptance may also be introduced in the design.

Simplicity of Return Design

Summary of outwards supplies and inward supplies akin to GSTR 3B shall constitute the main return. Annexure of invoices for outward supplies and inward supplies attracting reverse charge shall get populated/validated in the return. Taxpayer shall be given simple interface to upload the invoices. On filling the additional information required, if any, the return shall get generated on the IT system or on an offline tool to be provided.

Partial Payment of Tax

Partial payment of tax shall be allowed for B2C transaction but not for B2B transaction. In case no return is filed after uploading of the invoices by the seller, the uploaded invoices shall be treated as self-admitted liability and recovery made without going through the process of detailed adjudication. As the decision on partial payment shall have implication on both IT design and law, final decision would be taken after due consultation with the IT team and law committee during the detailing exercise on the return.

HSN

B2B invoice shall be uniformly generated at the line item level with atleast four digit of HSN declared for the same. This shall apply to all the taxpayers making B2B supply irrespective of the turnover.

Automatic Reversal of Credit

There shall not be any automatic reversal of input tax credit as it increases the IT design complexity and legally may be difficult to sustain. Recover of tax not paid or the reversal of input tax credit, as the case may be, shall be carried out in terms of clause (k) and (l).

Recovery from Seller and Reversal of Input Tax Credit in Exceptions

Misuse of input tax credit due to default in payment of tax by the seller shall be controlled primarily by recovery of tax from the seller however reversal of credit from buyer shall also be an option available with the revenue authorities to address situations like missing dealer, closer of business by supplier or supplier not having adequate assets etc. The reversal of credit from the seller shall be through a due process prescribed in the rules.

Preventive Measures for Controlling Input Tax Credit

To prevent misuse of input tax credit facility, adequate legal safeguards and IT facility shall be designed to block uploading of invoices in the subsequent month by a newly registered entity which has defaulted in paying taxes above a threshold limit. This would limit the possible damage and risk to the revenue. Similarly, safeguards would be built by blocking the upload of invoices for the existing units when they default in payment of tax above a threshold. Appropriate analytical tools would be built to identify high risk dealers, high risky defaulting dealers etc., and flag the same to the tax authorities for initiating compliance verification.

Content of the Return

Return shall be simplified by reducing the content/ information required to be filled in the return. It is suggested that the contents be examined in various categories such as information needed for calculating monthly liability, information needed for final settlement which can be part of annual return, information needed for audit and assessment can be part of the annual return, information which need not to be collected and any new information which may be needed to be collected due to new policy decisions.